IT SO HAPPENED . .

From Plough to Pulpit

by

ERIC CHALLONER

ISBN   0 9534295 0 4

Published by
Fairway Folio, Alsager, Cheshire
01270 874662
Typeset by Fairway Folio
Printed by Redwood Books, Trowbridge, Wilts

CONTENTS

ACKNOWLEDGEMENTS

First of all I want to thank God that after I accepted the challenge to write this book IT SO HAPPENED that three sisters were updating their computer and gave me their old Amstrad PCW256-just what I needed; thank you Kristy, Emma and Alison Grocott. I needed someone to teach me how to use my PCW, and I am indebted to Eric Willetts -a member of our church who was able and willing to come and teach me.

When I set out just over a year ago to collect material for the first chapters I was helped by my family, my brother Herbert, and sister Vera who had family pictures and childhood memories to share. Thanks to cousin Jack Adams who had done a careful genealogical study of the Challoner family. I used just a small part of this. To cousins Mary Mapes and Eileen Hamilton for pictures and stories about Grandpa and Grandma Mapes, To John and Peter for their encouragement and practical help. To Charles Tremlett my good friend from school days who reminded me of some of the things we did in those bygone days. I am indebted to John Williams and his daughter Lydia for help with some of the drawings, and to the Artist who painted the picture of the horses and ploughman on the front cover, which was from a Royal Agricultural Society Charity Christmas card. With the help of our local Library and the Charity, I've tried but failed to trace who, (if any), owns the copyright of this picture. I sincerely apologise if I have inadvertently infringed any copyright. I am thankful to Howard Booth who kindly wrote the Foreword. His friendship over the years, and his encouragement, help and wise advice have been very much appreciated.

Thanks also to Jack Sherratt for permission to use the photograph of miners at the pit head and to Dennis Doncaster for the photograph of the plough. Having laboriously produced pages of manuscript on floppy discs I discovered that my discs would not fit into the latest computers and after many enquiries was told that although it could be done it would be difficult. IT SO HAPPENED that Stuart Peel who prints our church notices each week had the latest equipment and was able and willing to take my manuscript and pictures and scan them into his machine, and prepared it all in detail, including the covers ready for publishing. This was a very big job and Stuart has amazed me with his professional skills and patience. I owe more to Stuart than anyone else. He and his wife Margaret have been most helpful, and I do thank them. Last, but not least, I thank Sheila who has spent hours by my side going through every word on the screen trying to correct spelling and 'ploughman's grammar' and checking stories for accuracy.

DEDICATION

I dedicate this book to my four grandchildren; Benjamin John, Kate Elizabeth, Emily Jane, and Arthur John (who arrived just in time to be included). May you each know that you are very special; that God loves you and has a plan and purpose for your life, as He had for mine.

FOREWORD

I arrived at Handsworth College, Birmingham in September 1948 to commence my training as a Methodist Minister. I soon discovered that the student occupying the study next door to me was a fellow named Eric Challoner. We became friends and quite early on found ourselves together in a Mission Band that went out from time to time leading evangelistic weekends in various Churches. From the very beginning I recognised in Eric a single-minded dedication to his Lord and to the call he had undoubtedly received into the Methodist Ministry. During our time there I came to know a certain delightful young lady whose name was Sheila who came to visit Eric now and again. This was the future Mrs. Challoner. When they married in 1950 there began a wonderful partnership which happily still continues.

When we left College our paths divided but we met up on occasions and I recall being a guest in their home for at least two and perhaps three Methodist Conferences. However it was retirement which brought us close together again. Eric and Sheila had retired to Alsager in 1983. In 1988 we had found a delightful bungalow in nearby Macclesfield but it was in a terrible state, especially the garden. Eric summoned up his friends and he and Sheila came over with them on numerous occasions to tame the wilderness and to discover the possibilities of a reasonable garden.

Then we started to be invited to do things together - weekends and conferences on health and healing; joint hosting for seniors holidays at Willersley Castle. All quite demanding but very enjoyable events. We seemed to work well together and complement each other. When Eric discussed with me the possibility of writing the story of his life I encouraged him to go right ahead. I knew something of the many events which had so happened during his life and particularly during his long years of ministry but as I have read some of the pages I have come to realise that I did not know the half. Things have happened to Eric which have made fascinating reading and they have just confirmed that Eric is as enthusiastic today as he ever was and that his ministry while different, still continues as is indicated by his Saturday morning telephone ministry when he calls up a wide circle of people all of whom value tremendously his prayerful, pastoral care.

Yes, there are many ordinary happenings recounted in these pages but some of the incidents can only be described as extraordinary and some I would even say are miraculous. Eric, supported every inch of the way by Sheila, has exercised a truly remarkable ministry which he describes in a sober and restrained manner which in no way exaggerates or "gilds the lily" but which tells it as it most certainly was. I hope that It So Happened will have many readers. No one could fail to be both held and inspired by it.

Howard Booth

6

INTRODUCTION

How do I - of all people - come to be writing this book now at the age of seventy nine having a memory that is more of a 'forgettery' and an old PC/Word Processor that can't spell? But I have a spirit that is full of joy and gratitude and I'm longing to be able to share with people, especially those near and dear to me, some of the lessons that I've learned and blessings I've received on life's journey.

I'm very conscious that so much has resulted from choices that I never made. I never chose to be born. I never chose my parents and what wonderful parents they were. The most important happenings in life were not of my choosing. But *IT SO HAPPENED*.

I never chose to go to a place called Measham as a young Methodist minister; I

Eric and Sheila at Dimmingsdale
Photographed on July 1st 1983 - the day before Eric's retirement.

7

was sent and *IT SO HAPPENED* that there I met Sheila Thirlby who became my wife. I believe that was a choice that was made in heaven and has proved to be the best choice of my life, for she has been such a wonderful friend, partner and example to me over the years. Without her we would not have had two sons - of whom we are proud - and their lovely families. Without her I wouldn't be writing this book.

I've tried to be as accurate as possible in telling my story and have consulted family, friends, what scanty records I have, the scrap books that Sheila has made and the photographs and tape recordings that we have. Some of these go back forty or more years, to when our sons were born. In the end, the best that I can do is to record events as I recall them but sometimes that recall mechanism has left gaps which I have done my best to fill. Where I've made mistakes and omissions - and there must be many - I ask forgiveness. However, from the very outset- and I know that this may sound pompous (but it is true) - the greatest help has come from God. There is no way that I could have tackled this book on my own.

God, who called me to be a preacher, indicated to me when my preaching days were over and then called me to write this book. His guiding spirit has enabled me to recall events and people long forgotten and to lead me to some fantastic people who helped me with this project in many practical ways; what is more, above all else, my faith has been strengthened, as a result of delving into the past, for I have seen so clearly the guiding hand of God.

I sincerely hope that my story will not only be interesting and at times - many times - cause a good laugh, but that the lessons that I've learned and share will be helpful.

I've included two maps and my 'family tree' on the following pages which readers may find useful.

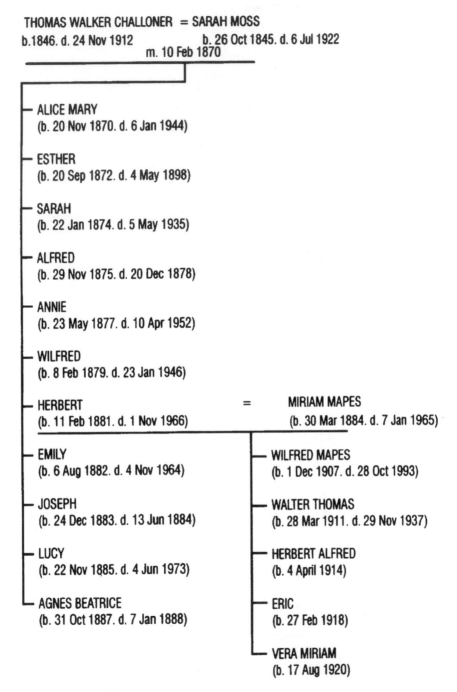

THOMAS WALKER CHALLONER = SARAH MOSS
b.1846. d. 24 Nov 1912   b. 26 Oct 1845. d. 6 Jul 1922
                    m. 10 Feb 1870

- ALICE MARY
  (b. 20 Nov 1870. d. 6 Jan 1944)

- ESTHER
  (b. 20 Sep 1872. d. 4 May 1898)

- SARAH
  (b. 22 Jan 1874. d. 5 May 1935)

- ALFRED
  (b. 29 Nov 1875. d. 20 Dec 1878)

- ANNIE
  (b. 23 May 1877. d. 10 Apr 1952)

- WILFRED
  (b. 8 Feb 1879. d. 23 Jan 1946)

- HERBERT   =   MIRIAM MAPES
  (b. 11 Feb 1881. d. 1 Nov 1966)   (b. 30 Mar 1884. d. 7 Jan 1965)

- EMILY   - WILFRED MAPES
  (b. 6 Aug 1882. d. 4 Nov 1964)   (b. 1 Dec 1907. d. 28 Oct 1993)

- JOSEPH   - WALTER THOMAS
  (b. 24 Dec 1883. d. 13 Jun 1884) (b. 28 Mar 1911. d. 29 Nov 1937)

- LUCY   - HERBERT ALFRED
  (b. 22 Nov 1885. d. 4 Jun 1973)   (b. 4 April 1914)

- AGNES BEATRICE   - ERIC
  (b. 31 Oct 1887. d. 7 Jan 1888)   (b. 27 Feb 1918)

                                 - VERA MIRIAM
                                   (b. 17 Aug 1920)

9

The New Pale, Manley

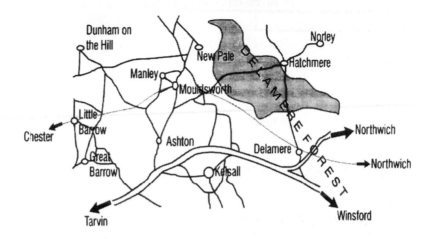

Long Lane Farm, Over Peover

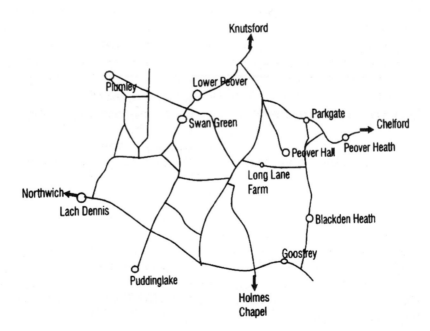

10

CHAPTER ONE

IN THE BEGINNING

Great is thy faithfulness, O God my Father,
There is no shadow of turning with thee;
Thou changest not, thy compassions, they fail not;
As thou hast been thou forever will be.
                                        Thomas O Chisholme.

The Midnight Rider

It was nearly midnight when the peace of the village of Little Barrow, was shattered by the sound of a galloping horse. It was not a highway robber, although they weren't unknown on the Chester-Warrington road in those days. Who then was it risking life and limb, galloping into the pitch darkness on his fiery steed? His name was Herbert Challoner. His mission was to win the hand of his sweetheart, Miriam Mapes, or, as she was always known, Minnie Mapes who lived at Little Barrow Hall. This was the very house where he had once lived with his father and mother, six sisters and one brother, moving in the year 1891 to Aston Grange between Frodsham and Warrington.

At that time young Minnie lived at Orchard Farm, Broomhill, near to Great Barrow, with her parents, Walter and Sarah Mapes, her sisters Jessie and Alice and her brothers Leonard, Walter and Archie. Minnie was the eldest girl and even at the age of seven was a great help in the home to her mother.

Just when Herbert Challoner returned to Little Barrow looking for his Minnie we don't know, but return he did and on horse back. The folk may not have heard him come but they certainly heard when he left. (Cousin Eileen Hamilton, daughter of mother's sister Jessie learnt this from her mother). His journeys weren't in vain, for in the early days of February 1907 Herbert Challoner was married to Miriam Mapes in Great Barrow church.

A home of their own

They were longing to have a home of their own but although they had a lot of love and great ambitions, they didn't have a lot of this world's goods. Herbert, being one of a family of ten, couldn't expect much from his parents, but they did their best and gave him a horse and cart, which proved to be a valuable asset. Minnie's 'dowry' was six young heifers. They were fortunate in being able to rent a smallholding at Winwick near Warrington.

Their first year was very hard because they had no money. To go to a farm without money is not like going to an ordinary job where you would have a wage. They had no income because they had no milk to sell or crops to harvest. But they did have a horse and cart and father was soon looking for work. He went down to the canal lock which wasn't far away and discovered barges coming from Liverpool loaded with horse manure for the local farmers. He offered his services and was given the job of carting this manure. These farms were well known for growing potatoes.

When the potatoes were harvested he carted these to the barge boats that had brought the manure and loaded them for Liverpool. It was hard work but he was never afraid of that and soon discovered that this was a good source of income which enabled him to employ a man and to spend money on the farm. He saw how

Grandmother Mapes with Mother, Wilfred and Walter. 1912

well the potatoes did in that area so he ploughed, planted and grew an excellent crop himself. He and Minnie went there in 1907 with his horse and cart and six heifers and in less than six years had established himself on the farm and, what is more important, they had three healthy lads; Wilfred, Walter and Herbert.

Long Lane Farm

It was then that he began looking round for a bigger place to rent. He saw an advert in the paper - probably the Warrington Guardian- stating that Long Lane Farm, Over Peover (pronounced 'Peever'), part of the Peover Hall Estate, owned by a Mr Peel, was to be rented with vacant possession in February 1914. There were a number of applicants but he was selected.

And so it was that my father and mother, with Wilfred, aged six, Walter four and baby Herbert six months, together with three horses, cattle, farm implements and furniture, moved to Long Lane Farm, Over Peover, near Knutsford. Mother certainly would have her hands full with two little lads and a baby. Father too had his work cut out moving in February. There was ploughing to be done and seeds to be sown.

Foden Dean

One of their very first visitors was a neighbouring farmer, Foden Dean, who came to give the family a welcome. He very generously offered father a man, a plough and a team of horses for a week or more to help him catch up with his Spring ploughing. Father gladly accepted. As he was leaving Mr Dean said, "By the way, Mr Challoner, are you a churchman?" Thinking that he meant "Are you Church of England?" Father replied, "No, I'm chapel". He then shook father's hand and said "Come to our chapel at Snelson with the family next Sunday and then come to Newhall and have tea with us". That visit and invitation not only introduced the Challoner family to Snelson chapel, but to Foden Dean and his wife. The Deans had no children, but they had a nephew, John Johnson, whom they treated as a son and who, with his wife Connie, became the closest of friends with my parents.

Their son Dean and his wife Muriel later became our close friends as did their two sons Martyn and Kevin with their children together with Dean's sisters Betty and Mary. So that very first visit of Foden Dean to Long Lane Farm resulted in my having a close link with five generations of lovely people whose friendship has enriched my life down through the years.

A 'Chariot Race'

In those days the main form of travel was by horse and float. Father was the very proud owner of a chestnut mare, Tarta. He loved to tell stories about this mare and the following was one of his favourites.

One day he took mother to see her parents at Little Barrow Hall - a journey of about twenty miles. On the return journey, not far from Northwich, they were about to be overtaken by another horse and float. As it began to gallop past, Tarta increased her speed. The other driver, who they learned later was a butcher from Knutsford, whipped his horse and a real race began. Father just gave Tarta a loose rein and she left the butcher's horse far behind. Some time later this same man came to Long Lane to see if father would sell Tarta. Father was very reluctant to part with this chestnut mare but the offer was so generous that he accepted. Before the butcher took Tarta away, father said "Whatever you do you must never hit this horse"; and the butcher promised that he wouldn't.

Less than a month later this same man came to see father and asked if he would mind having Tarta back. When father asked why, he said that the horse had "run away" smashed the float and that he himself had been nearly killed. "Did you touch her with your whip ?" father asked. He confessed that he had. "I wanted to find out just how fast she would go, but I never expected anything like this to happen". Although Father was glad to have his favourite mare back he was very angry about what happened and said Tarta was never the same horse afterwards.

Little Eric is born

The family had been at Long Lane Farm for four years when I arrived on February 27th 1918 - the final year of World War One. My eldest brother was called Wilfred Mapes Challoner, then Walter Thomas (Walter after Grandfather Mapes and Thomas after Grandfather Challoner), then Herbert Alfred (Herbert after father and Alfred being a Challoner name). When I arrived they only gave me one name. I was told that because of food rationing mother had to fill in forms for each person giving the full name; so I was given just one short name. I'm sure that my parents must have been disappointed when another boy arrived. However, two years later they were blessed with a lovely little daughter whom they called Vera Miriam. She was given two names because food rationing had ended!

My first school

When I was five and old enough to go to school, it was decided that because two miles was a long way for a little lad to walk, I should wait until I was six. At the end of the lane, in London Road Lodge, lived the Booths with their two sons Walmsley and Daniel. Walmsley was my age and came to school with me. Dan was a baby with red hair and his mother said that she always knew when it was going to rain for "our Dan's hair curls". Further along the road we called at a farm for two sisters whose father had a severe drink problem, causing great problems for the girls and their mother.

You might well ask, "Just what sort of parents did he have to let their little Eric set out each day on this journey?" The fact is that in those days no one for a moment thought there was any danger and I certainly didn't.

Eric (front right) in the school garden at Lower Peover. The church is in the centre with the infant's school on the left and the junior school on the right.

14

The very old church

The school itself was a Church of England school with a long history going back to the 17th century. On one side stands the ancient and famous Warren de Tabley Arms Hotel, now known as the Bells of Peover. On the other side is the old 12th century church, which is surrounded by grave stones. Every day that I came to school I had to enter the church yard through a gate close to Cragg's shop where we could buy a small bag of aniseed balls for a halfpenny. These were brown-coated sugar balls with an aniseed in the centre. Because it was a Church of England school, the vicar visited us regularly to take prayers and on special days all the school had to march across to the church for a service.

It was a most unusual and interesting place inside. The pews were raised from the floor and each had a narrow door which had to be opened to get in and then shut.

The vicar explained to us that in the early days of the church there was no heating so the pews were raised from the ground for warmth and that in the coldest days the farmers brought straw and gave a good 'bedding' of straw in each pew - just like they did in the shippon for the cows to lie on. On one of the pillars there was a wooden shelf and we were told that in the past the church members would bring a loaf to church each Sunday to put on the shelf and these loaves were given to the poor during the week. This throws light on social conditions at that time.

How a young farmer chose his wife

The church contains a very old oak chest which has a very heavy lid. The vicar told us that in the olden days when a young farmer was looking for a wife, before he proposed he would bring her into the church. The vicar at that time would unlock the chest and the girl would be asked to lift this great heavy lid with one hand. If she could do it she was considered strong enough to be a farmer's wife. I expect that today we would think it a foolish idea but in those days many of the farms were small and the work would be done by the farmer and his wife. If she was not strong she would not be able to do the work and if she could not do the work, she would be unhappy and so would he. Whether we agree or not at least they did consider before marriage what might be involved.

A 'Mixed Infant'

Margaret, Eric and Vera resting after playing in the field.

I was a 'Mixed Infant' and Mrs Booth was our teacher. Our classroom was the old school house. I don't think that it would have been the original one but it was certainly very old and separate from the main building. There was a coal-fired stove at one side, with a big strong wire guard round it. If we got wet, which we often did, we were allowed to hang

15

our wet things on this guard to dry. They did soon dry, but it caused a bit of a smell.

One day we had some excitement! A girl screamed because a mouse had run over her foot. Other girls started to scream and the lads began a mouse hunt. They managed to catch it and Mrs Booth put it outside. Poor little mouse! However there was not a lot of excitement in school at first for me. After I had walked two miles my little legs were tired and the hot stove made me sleepy and I often found it hard to keep awake. On a nice day Mrs Booth would sometimes take us for a Nature walk along the cobblestone road (it is still cobblestones seventy years later) and we had to collect leaves, berries and perhaps a feather which we placed on a table when we returned and Mrs Booth would help us to identify them. Then we would make drawings in our notebooks together with names.

Bad lads!

At seven we moved up into the 'big school' where Mrs Dawson taught. She was the wife of the Headmaster. In those days if you did wrong you got the cane. I only had it once all the time I was there. During the lunch break we were playing in the school field, next to a field with tents in it. A young couple went into one of these tents and two of us crept through a gap in the hedge and quietly pulled up the tent pegs, causing the tent to collapse on the couple inside. We ran back to school but the fellow followed us and reported the matter to the head master, who came into our class and enquired who was responsible. We both owned up for he said that no one would be allowed to go home until he had found the culprits. We had to stand out in front of the class and he announced that we would be severely caned after school. We were taken to his room and he took a bamboo cane out of the cupboard. I went first, held my right hand out and he gave me a hard smack and then another on my left hand. It was very painful and made my fingers swell, but I didn't cry. When I got home and told my father what had happened he was angry with me and warned me that if I ever got the cane again I would "get my back-side smacked". It did me no harm but taught me a lesson that I didn't forget.

Remember, it is all down in the book!

Incidentally just 71 years after that event, I went with Sheila to the Bells of Peover for lunch and afterwards we went across to the school. When the headmistress knew that I had been a pupil there she kindly invited us into her office and found the register for the year 1924. There she found written "Eric Challoner; Father, Herbert Challoner, farmer: Long Lane Farm, Over Peover". She then got the Punishment Register out and we saw page after page of punishments but she couldn't find my name there. Afterwards I thought that she must have been looking in the wrong year. As we left the school that afternoon I thought "Fancy keeping a record of my sin in that school register".

There was another time when I was in trouble and this time the Headmaster came to my rescue. We were having a games session in the school yard one afternoon

16

and one of the things that we had to do was to 'leap frog' over a row of scholars (one at a time). As I went over the last one he fell forward and I went with him and went head first into the wall making a nasty gash in my forehead, After giving me first aid, Mrs Dawson took me round to the School House (to me the Holy of Holies). She gave me a lovely orange drink and told me to lie down until after school and Mr Dawson would take me home. The only means of transport that he had was his bicycle and he took me home on his cross bar.

On another occasion I was given a ride on the cross bar of a policeman's bike. Some of father's sheep had been chased and savaged by a dog. I had seen a dog in the field but I didn't actually see it chasing the sheep. Father reported this to the police and when the officer arrived he asked me to describe the dog. At that time I collected cigarette cards and had a series on dogs. I found the dog's picture, an Airedale, and said I thought I knew where it came from. It was then that he took me on his bike to identify this dog at a kennel. I wasn't happy because the dog was found guilty and destroyed. This upset me very much but father told me that once a dog had killed a sheep and tasted blood, it could never be trusted again and had to be 'put to sleep'. That made me feel less guilty.

World without Television

I suppose that it's difficult for any young person today to try and imagine a world without TV or radio. My granddaughter Kate asked "Grandpa, whatever did you find to do?" I told her there were lots of things that we did and what's more I don' t remember ever being bored. I suppose the reason is that we so often made our own games and these continually changed, following a pattern throughout the year. There would be a period when marbles were popular, then conkers when horse chestnuts were ready and in winter skipping and hopscotch which helped to keep us warm.

I was lucky of course living on a farm, for there were so many things for me to do. I always had animals to care for and my own garden. Again, when it was harvest time we didn't need any games to amuse us, for we rode on the lorries going into the field to bring in the sheaves of corn and hay. After the corn had been cut we were able to make little houses with the sheaves and hide in them. They were for the most part simple games but great fun and cost little or nothing.

A whisker without a cat

One day Wilfred arrived home with a box containing a kit for making a wireless. I forget all that was in it, but I do remember it included a 'cat's whisker', a crystal, a metal rod, quite a lot of wire and a pair of head phones. (This cat's whisker was not from one of our farm cats but a special piece of fine wire which was controlled by a knob). He assembled it in the sitting room, overlooking the back garden and made a small hole at the bottom of the window then threaded two wires through - one for the earth and the other for the aerial. He drove the metal rod (which was about two feet long) into the garden and fastened the earth wire to it. Then he took the aerial wire up the side of the house, above the bedroom window and fastened it to the wall and then to the top branch of a tall tree. When all the parts were assembled he sent me into the garden with a bucket of water to pour over his earth rod (this, he said, was to help it to earth!). Then came the critical bit. With his headphones on and his hand on the knob of the cat's whisker, which was in contact with the crystal, he carefully moved it round until it touched the right spot and picked up a radio signal. There was great excitement when Wilfred got his first signal. He yelled "I've got it, I've got it", We all wanted to have a listen and although the sound was rather distant, we could clearly hear it. To us this was a miracle of science.

Washing clothes

I am afraid that for Mother and others who worked in the house there was not a lot of time for games of any sort. I'm

Mrs Briscall with husband Hughie

thinking particularly of little Mrs Briscall, Mother's washer-woman, who came every Monday to do the family wash and spent all day doing it. In the corner of the wash house was the boiler, which held about twenty gallons of water. It was built in a brick frame over a fire in a grate. On Monday morning at about six, father would light the fire in the grate, the boiler having been filled the night before. Mrs Briscall, who lived in one of the cottages across the field, came at eight o'clock. The first thing that she did was to put two buckets of the boiling water into a dolly tub, which was a galvanised tub about the size of a dust bin. To this she would add sufficient cold water to give the right temperature. There were no washing machines or spin dryers. All the action was done by little Mrs Briscall and her dolly peg. This was like a three legged low wooden stool, which had a hole drilled through the centre and a wooden shaft about three feet long pushed into it with another piece of wood across the top which made a handle to hold. She used this to agitate the clothes by giving the dolly peg sharp twists until the clothes were clean. Then they had to be put through a heavy mangle into another dolly tub for rinsing, lifted out and mangled again and then hung out to dry. Mrs B. was so short she found it difficult to reach the line and had to take the wooden

steps out if no one else was there to help her. The pegs she used had been made by gypsies who came round selling them.

When the clothes were dry they had to be brought in and ironed. There was no electricity then so she used several flat irons. These were placed on a special ledge on the kitchen grate until they were hot enough. Care had to be taken to get them to the right temperature; too hot they would singe; too cool they wouldn't iron. Great care had to be taken to see that the irons were clean. There were no easy care materials then and to get a good finish starch had to be used. A bowl of it would be prepared then shirt cuffs and collars and other special whites were dipped in it, wrung out, then ironed carefully. At the end of a big washing day, when she had washed all the clothes, sheets, towels, table cloths etc. for a family of seven Mrs Briscall would make her weary way home across the fields and prepare a meal for a hungry husband and two hungry lads.

Mrs Briscall had earned her bed!

Mothers help in the kitchen

I reckon that during the first ten years of my life I lost about two and a half years' schooling - at least I was away from school for that time. I had been a premature baby and Mother had a job to rear me. I suppose that she had to be extra careful with me and as already mentioned I didn't start school till I was six. I had double pneumonia when I was eight and spent over a year and a half at home. Looking back now, I must say that those years 'helping' Mother in the home weren't wasted. She was always busy and I loved to watch her baking bread. She had a big bread bowl and would put the dough with the yeast in it by the side of the fire and cover it with a cloth while it rose to twice the size. When she baked a cake, I liked to scrape the basin and eat the remains of the mixture. If she had any pastry left, she would let me make a currant pasty, or a jam tart. This experience benefited me later in life.

Having no gas or electricity Mother had to do all her cooking over the fire, or in the fire-oven. She produced some good meals for the family of seven and in addition had extra mouths to feed at harvest time and when we threshed the corn or sheared the sheep.

The Doctor gets a shock

It was at this time when I was seriously ill with pneumonia that a very funny thing happened. I had to spend weeks in bed during the winter, and longed to get up and go out especially when my brother Herbert announced that one of our gill ferrets had given birth to five little ones. They are lovely little creatures when

they are able to run about, and I persuaded him to put them in a shoe box and bring them to my bed. I tried to keep them out of mother's sight for she didn't like them, especially in the house. But they were great fun. I would put them into the sleeve of my pyjamas, and they would scramble up one sleeve and

across my chest and down the other. They enjoyed this, and so did I until the day Dr. Surridge from Knutsford arrived unannounced, and mother brought him upstairs before I could box my little pets. I don't think he was very fond of children, or their pets, and certainly not after what happened next. With stethoscope at the ready he announced, "Now, young man, let me listen to that chest of yours." So saying he pulled back the bed clothes and uncovered a nest of little ferrets on my chest. My mother screamed "Eric" and the doctor swore, and waited till I had put them in their box before he listened to my chest. I think that if we had listened to his heart at that time it would have been beating faster than usual. However, the good thing about that visit was that he said to mother "If that lad is fit to play with ferrets, he's fit to get up" which I did. But doctor Surridge never forgot that visit - neither did I.

The blessings of the family

Today the average size of a family is four. I am glad that I was one of a bigger family and we have always been good friends; what is more we have remained so. I can't say we didn't have squabbles and arguments at home - that's all part of family life. Father was strict with us and his word was law, but although we knew that if we did wrong we would be punished, we loved and respected him.

When we were all together as a family at mealtimes, we all had our own place at the table with Father at one end and Mother at the other. Father carved the meat with a very sharp carving knife and kept a sharpening steel near, in order to put an 'edge' on it before cutting the meat. Anyone who used Father's knife for anything else was in trouble. He always said grace before a meal, a practice that we have tried to follow. At that time it was something that was done much more often, but sadly, not so often now.

This simple act of saying grace was not only a means of acknowledging our indebtedness to God but also of bonding us together as a family, and we never began to eat until father had said grace. Such meal times were special.

Eric in more trouble!

After spending the winter away from school because of sickness, it was decided that when spring came I would be able to go back. During the Easter holidays I collected some frog spawn in a large jar and looked forward to this developing into tadpoles and then hopefully into little frogs. I was keen to watch this development but mother was not so keen so I had to find some place to hide them. I got an old washing up bowl and filled it with water, put the spawn in it and put it on a shelf in the cellar. Each day after school I would go and have a secret look, and slowly the little tadpoles began to form. However it was too slowly for a young impatient lad, who had many other interests, and I forgot to go down the cellar for a while. This was a big mistake.

We had no fridge or freezer in those days, but as the cellar was always very cool, mother kept things down there. One day she had a filled a bucket with eggs and covered them with a preservative called water glass, and went to take it down the cellar steps. When she opened the door at the top of the steps she was greeted by an army of little frogs. It's a miracle she never dropped the bucket of eggs on top of them. When I got home from school that night she was waiting for me, and asked me to go down the cellar. I couldn't believe my eyes; there seemed to be almost a hundred miniature frogs, many of them on the steps. Each seemed to have a spring in its back legs that enabled it to jump almost a foot high. "Now I want you to catch every one of those little frogs and take them out of my cellar" said mother. I hadn't found it easy to catch five little ferrets and put them into their box, so how was I going to catch all these little frogs. They are marvellous little creatures, so wonderfully made, and so very agile, and I knew that I would have great difficulty in catching them without hurting them.

This is what I did - and looking back I now marvel at my ingenuity as a lad of nine. I got a big bucket and put about two inches of water in the bottom, to stop them from jumping. I wet a big square duster, and wrung it out. Having managed to get several frogs together I would drop the damp duster on them and scoop them up and drop them in the bucket. When I had collected them all, I took them to the little pond where I had originally found the spawn, and so 'completed the cycle'!

CHAPTER TWO

LONG LANE FARM, OVER PEOVER.

Through all the changing scenes of life,
In trouble and in joy,
The praises of my God shall still
My heart and tongue employ.
Nahum Tate & Nicholas Brady.

Auntie Jessie Haswell

One of our favourite visitors at Long Lane was Auntie Jessie Haswell. She was not really our auntie but a close friend of Grandma Mapes. Her home was in Chester where she had a café and cake shop and her cakes were special. When she came to our house she was always busy, either baking or sewing, and with a family of five children - four of them hungry lads - and a hard working father, there was always plenty of baking to do.

One thing that I remembered about her baking was that she was always very clean and tidy, washing her hands after each operation and also the baking things, so that before the cakes were baked the pots and pans were washed and

Eric re-visiting Long Lane Farm. June 1986.

*King Charles'
Tower, Chester*

put away. She was also an artist with her needle and thread, skilfully weaving beautiful pictures on tapestry for chair backs and bottoms, fire screens and framed pictures. I know of many people who proudly possess one of Auntie Jessie Haswell's masterpieces.

A holiday in Chester with Herbert

It was a special treat for Herbert and me when she invited us both to come and stay with her in Chester. She lived just by the Grosvenor Park gate, so it was very handy for us; we could run out through the front door, across the park to the river or the famous Roman Walls. There weren't the crowds in those days and we two lads could go off on our own to explore this ancient city. However it was much better for us when Auntie Jessie Haswell came with us (we always gave her this full title for mother had a sister Jessie who was our real auntie).

She was born in Chester in the days of Queen Victoria. She had spent all her life there and could tell us such a lot about the different places that we went to. I remember standing on King Charles's Tower, on the walls, and Auntie pointing out the site of ancient battle fields in the distance. At the base of the tower was a large cage in which they used to lock up wrong-doers as a deterrent to others.

The fiery preacher

On the Sunday Auntie Jessie Haswell took us to the Presbyterian Church. I remember the service well. I don't remember what the preacher said but I do remember how he said it and how he frightened me to death. It was so different from Snelson, my own chapel that I loved. We sat in pews with doors and there was a door on the pulpit. A man carrying a Bible climbed up the pulpit steps and put the Bible in its place, then came down and the minister, wearing a black flowing gown, took his place and the pulpit door was shut. He was Welsh and passionate, and the longer he preached the louder he preached. He seemed to keep looking at me and I moved up close to Auntie wondering what would happen if he got out! I was glad when the service was over and we could go home. As we passed him at the door he seemed much less angry, in fact quite friendly, but I did wish that he hadn't shouted so loudly from the pulpit. I wonder just what I would have thought if someone had told me then that one day I would be a minister. I hope I never frightened any little lad as he frightened me that Sunday. But I soon forgot this, for when we got home Auntie produced a scrumptious Sunday dinner. What was it that made Aunt Jessie Haswell so special to a little lad of eight? She made us feel that we were important, giving us her undivided attention and she tried to see things from our point of view.

Grandfather and Grandmother Mapes.

Grandfather and Grandmother Mapes lived at Little Barrow Hall and Herbert and I loved to go on the train from Knutsford to stay with them. I have many memories of those holidays. I remember looking through the bedroom window, about midnight, and hearing and seeing a steam train coming. When the stoker

Little Barrow Hall

opened the boiler door it seemed not only to light the cabin, but the sky too. It looked like a dragon breathing fire and steam into the darkness of the night.

When our stay included a Sunday we would go to church. Grandfather would get us up early. There was no bathroom or toilet or even taps in the house so we had to wash in the back kitchen, where there was a stone slab on which was placed a bowl. Although there was a pump in the yard, we had to get the water to wash from a water butt into which the rain water ran from the roof. Grandfather said that this was much better than the pump water for washing in. It was 'softer', which meant that it had less lime in it, and provided a much better lather with very little soap - but, my word, it was cold. We had to strip to our waist and when we had finished Grandpa would inspect us, then, in a very serious tone of voice, he said "You know my lads, you can't go to church dirty."

Going to Church with Charlie.

I didn't enjoy getting ready for church, but I did enjoy the ride in the trap that was pulled by Charlie, Grandpa's white pony. When Charlie moulted, losing his winter coat, he trotted along the road and we - in the trap - would find Charlie's hair drifting on to us. Grandfather was well prepared for this.

As soon as we drew up near the church, Charlie was tethered to a post, Grandfather produced a big clothes brush and we were all brushed. We then all followed him into the church to the Mapes' pew which was at the front near the pulpit. I wondered if we were going to have a fiery sermon from the Rector like we had at Aunt Jessie Haswell's church. I'm glad to say we didn't.

The Rector who came to Church in his football boots.

The rector was the Rev. Thomas Jenkins who, years later after his wife died, married my mother's widowed sister, Aunt Al. Like Grandfather, he was a very keen sportsman and played cricket for Barrow. In his early days before he came to Barrow and whilst he was still a curate, he played rugby for Wales. There is a story told about him - in fact I think it was Tom himself who told us (we called him Tom after he married Aunt Al). One Saturday afternoon, he had both a wedding and a football match. He arranged the wedding to follow the match but there was some delay in the game which meant that he was late for the wedding. He rushed from the match in his boots and shorts and rugby shirt, into the church vestry where the verger, who was anxiously waiting, helped him to put on his cassock over everything. He went clattering down the aisle in his football boots to meet the bride. You could say that he had two matches that day.

Grandfather was born in Norfolk. He was the son of Leonard Mapes who was a gamekeeper, and retired with his wife Emily to the keeper's cottage at Long Green near Little Barrow. He lived to be ninety two. As well as having a farm to look after Grandfather had other jobs. He was district agent for Hadfields Fertiliser, the school attendance officer and rate collector. Herbert and I enjoyed going round with him in the trap. Sometimes when folk didn't want to pay their rates they hid from him.

He was also a keen cricketer and I remember watching him play for Barrow when he was seventy two. At that time he was allowed a runner. I once saw his runner get run out after running when grandfather had shouted "No". Grandfather was so angry with him that, with his bat above his head, he chased the lad all the way to the pavilion and nearly caught him! Everybody said that was the best part of the match.

The train that didn't stop

I laugh every time I think of the following incident. On Saturday afternoons, when Chester were playing at home Grandpa would go with two of his friends from Mickle Trafford to watch the match. After the match they would go to a pub for a pint and a bite and then come home on the train. The first station was Mickle Trafford, followed by Barrow and then Mouldsworth.

This particular time the railway authorities had decided to cut out the Mickle Trafford stop, making Barrow the first. Whether they had drunk more than one pint, or never been told about the alteration, Grandfather's friends got out at Barrow and he came on to Mouldsworth! About seven o'clock that night we had a 'phone call from the station master, who knew us well. He was laughing his head off, "I've got a Mr Walter Mapes here and he would like one of you to take him home to Little Barrow". It was Walter and I who went. Grandpa was cross with himself, but he said it was worth it when he thought of his two mates having to walk back to Mickle Trafford.

Grandma

Grandfather was disappointed that Grandma was not very interested in sport. Sometimes, on a warm summer evening she would watch a game of cricket, especially when the rector, who was then the Rev. Mr Arnold was playing. She had a high regard for him and she loved his sister, Miss Arnold, who had a great influence on her life and on the lives of many people in the parish.

Grandfather gets two surprises

In those days husbands tended to 'hold the purse strings', so when Grandma wanted to buy anything, she had to ask her husband for the money and to tell him what she wanted to buy. This made it very difficult when she wanted to buy him a present, for it to be a surprise. However, Grandma was very shrewd. She knew that he always wanted a really good pair of binoculars and decided to give him a pair for his birthday. So she went to the famous jewellers in Chester, Butt and Co., spoke to the manager and told him she wanted to give her husband a pair of binoculars. She wanted it to be a surprise but would like him to have some choice in the matter. She asked that a box of three be packed up with a letter from the manager stating that a good friend had ordered them to be sent for Mr Mapes to choose a pair and to send the other two back. You can well imagine how very surprised and pleased Grandfather was and how very puzzled too. He made his choice and took the other two pairs back.

But, he was to have another surprise. About one month after his birthday he received a bill from Butt and Co. for his binoculars, with a note from the manager explaining what had happened and trusting that he was pleased with the 'gift' from his wife.

I loved being with Grandpa and Grandma Mapes but I feel so sad to think that lots of young people these days often lose touch with their grandparents when their parents are divorced. It is both a tragedy for them and for their grandparents.

Reflections on my father's influence on my life.

In these last few weeks I have been probing into the deep recesses of my mind and I have uncovered treasures that have been lost and truths that have been hidden, and I am truly thankful. I have come to realise as never before, the significance of those early days at Long Lane Farm at Over Peover and the vital role that my father played in my life. Mother was the one who was always closest to me. I suppose one of the reasons was that from birth I was a physically weak child and she had to take special care of me. Father was not so close until after he had retired and I had left home, and especially after mother died. Of course he spent most of his waking hours outside working and always seemed to be very busy. When he was working with the men, he liked to take a lead, working hard and expecting them to work hard too. But he was always fair and never asked them to do what he did not do himself. He was respected not only by his workmen but by his neighbouring farmers too.

Was father a 'religious' man?

I'm not sure if I would have known what was meant by that question then. I suppose one 'religious' thing that he did was to say grace at meals. At the time I didn't regard it as being 'religious', but something that he had always done. He never ever spoke to me about prayer; it was mother who taught me to say my prayers. However, it made a big impression on me when, one night, I ran into my parents bedroom after they had gone to bed and father, in his night-shirt, was kneeling at his side of the bed saying his prayers. He never told me that it was wrong to swear but I never heard him once say a swear word and when he was present the men didn't swear either, although I don't think he ever told them not to.

Father made Sunday a day that was different

He didn't say we must go to chapel on Sunday. He went himself and we did what he did. He never gave us a lecture on what we should do - or not do - on Sunday. He saw to it that Sunday was a day that was different. On the farm, of course, there was always work to be done, cows to be milked, animals to be fed, dairy things to be washed and sterilised with steam which meant a boiler had to be lit.

But no job that was not essential was done. Father liked to have as much of the day off as possible, and he saw to it that the men had their time off too. This also applied to holidays. Farm workers at that time got very little time off for holidays with pay, but father made sure that those who worked for him did. Some neighbouring farmers were angry, saying that he was creating a dangerous precedent.

I know that when I was older and working on the farm we were very dependent at harvest time on fine weather in order to get the corn cut and carted. The neighbouring farmers would all be busy on a fine Sunday and they thought father was mad for allowing his men and machines to be idle just because it was Sunday. Father never attempted to give a 'religious' reason for what he did. What he would say was something like this, "You please yourself, but I have never harvested on a Sunday. When I and my men have worked hard for six days, we need a day off and what is more, over the years, I have never 'lost out' through making Sunday a day that is different". He was right too. In war time when the government ordered the munitions workers and plane builders, during a period of special need, to work seven days a week, it was soon discovered that production fell so they went back to a six day week.

In the home, too, Sunday was a day that was different. We never had a Sunday newspaper, but the one paper we did have and read on Sunday was the Christian Herald. When Vera and I were too young to go to chapel on Sunday night, father stayed in to look after us and would read a serial story from it, which we enjoyed.

I suppose today folk would suggest that I had been imprisoned in a very restrictive system. In reply I would say Sunday was always a day that I really enjoyed. It was special and different, and because of this it not only made Monday a day that was different but the rest of the week too. So I am thankful to my father for the part that he played in helping me to lay a foundation for a life that has brought such joy and happiness to me.

The big move

In 1930, having been at Long Lane for some fifteen years, and now joined by both Wilfred and Walter, with Herbert ready to leave school, father decided that the time had come for him to look for a bigger farm. It was then that he heard that a new tenant was wanted for a farm called the New Pale at Manley, situated on the edge of Delamere Forest.

Delamere comes from the French 'Forêt de la mare' - that is Forest of lakes, or meres. The name first appeared in 1248. The word 'pale' means enclosure and in 1337 an enclosure called the Old Pale was made to keep out the deer. Another circular clearing of 340 acres was made and in 1653 this was to become a farm, the New Pale. It was part of the Duchy of Lancaster estate, 'Crown Land', which meant it belonged to the king. The Old Pale had been farmed by the Frith family for many years and the New Pale by the Harrisons, the tenancy having been handed on from father to son. The last Harrison had no sons, so that is why the Crown agent was looking for a new tenant.

A Royal farm

There were many applicants from all over the country, and a shortlist of eight was drawn up. Father was on this, and had to meet the Crown Commissioners at the Abbey Arms, Oakmere. After this he was on a shortlist of two. Now when father heard that the other farmer was John Frith, from Sudlow farm, Knutsford, a well known farmer in the area who was related to the Friths of the Old Pale, he felt that there was very little chance of his getting the farm. With the letter informing him that he was on a shortlist, was a notice that the chief agent of the Crown, Mr Carter-Jonas, would like to come to look over Long Lane and meet the family. This was arranged for one Saturday.

The Crown Commissioner's visit and verdict

There was much activity on the farm before this important visitor came. To me it felt as though we were going to have a visit from the King himself. He came and gladly accepted mother's invitation to have dinner at twelve, the time we always had dinner. We had a large farmhouse kitchen with a big table in it and mother prepared a meal fit for royalty. The agent sat at the table with father at one end, mother at the other, together with Wilfred (22), Walter (18), Herbert, (15) Eric (11) and Vera (8). When the agent left he said that he would be writing to father in the next few days.

They must have been anxious days, particularly for father and mother. When the letter arrived it informed father that they were happy to tell him that the Crown Commissioners had decided to give him the tenancy of the New Pale. Father always said that the thing that had impressed the agent most of all was not what he saw on the farm, but what he saw at the table, the meal mother prepared and the family of four boys, all interested in farming. I am sure that he was also impressed with our little sister whom we all made a fuss of.

The pain of parting

When I had got over the excitement of father getting the tenancy of the New Pale, I began to think with sadness of having to leave Long Lane, the place where I was born, the only home that I had ever known and where I had been so happy. I was sad to be leaving Lower Peover school and my friends there and Snelson chapel. I thought about my garden where I had grown my own flowers and my very first radishes. I didn't like radishes but I did like growing them because they were colourful and grew quickly. I remember too my very first cauliflower and how I cut it and proudly took it indoors. It was the size of a big orange, and father told me that it would have grown three times as big if I had left it. However mother said she would cook it just for me, and make some cheese sauce to put on it. I think that was one of the most enjoyable dishes that I ever had, and cauliflower cheese is still one of my favourite meals.

Memories in a box

I wondered just what I could do to help me remember this place that was so dear to me. I decided to take a bit of it with me. So I asked mother for a small screw top metal box, then I went on a nostalgic walk round the farm to those places that meant most to me and at each place took a spoonful of the soil. There was soil from my very own garden, there was soil from underneath the old oak tree, where Vera and I used to play. There was soil from beneath the tree that grew by the pond; a pond where waterhens nested, and where we had watched the baby waterhens grow. It was this tree that Herbert and I loved to climb. There were other places too from where I took this precious soil to put into my box - my box of happy memories.

The girl I left behind

When we are older we tend to forget that the hearts of boys and girls can be very tender, relationships very meaningful and possibly full of anguish. It is probably even more true today with all the media and peer pressure on young people to rush into such relationships. I remember so well my first love and I remember too, one Friday afternoon when I was in Mr Dawson's class. It was winter and often on a Friday afternoon we would have country dancing. Now at that time in our class there was a lovely girl called Margaret. I was a bit shy and although I sometimes had a word with her, I never thought that she was interested in me, or knew just how I felt about her. So what made this particular Friday afternoon so very special?

During the country dancing we often had different partners, but on this day each girl was given a yellow ribbon and when the music started she had to give one end of her ribbon to the boy of her choice. Margaret walked straight over and offered me her ribbon, inviting me to be her partner. That was a special moment for me, and I believe that it was for her. It seemed that we both had felt the same way about each other, but neither of us had let the other know. Now the very sad ending to this story is that all this happened just as we were about to leave and I'm afraid I left my Margaret behind!

CHAPTER THREE

THE NEW PALE, MANLEY. 1929-1934

We know not what the future holds,
But we do know who holds the future.
Willis J. Ray.

The business of moving

The business of moving, for me, has always been a traumatic experience and a real upheaval in life. As a minister, one of the drawbacks of the job is having to move quite often. It is not as often now as it was when I first entered the ministry, but it never seems to get any easier. When I think of what it means for ministers to move house, I think just what it must have been like for my father as he moved from Long Lane Farm, Over Peover, to the New Pale. He had to think of the crops in the fields that were in different stages of growth and putting a value on them for his successor. He had to think of the cows, some forty or more, all having to be fed and milked on the morning of the move and again in the afternoon in a strange shippon (cowshed) with each cow in a strange stall. Cows are creatures of habit and they like their own stall. If disturbed they do not 'let their milk down'. In addition to the cows there were the pigs, big ones and little ones, hens, rabbits, cats (several), a dog and ferrets. Then there was the hay and straw, all the farm implements - ploughs, harrows, drills and rollers etc.

All these had to be transported as well as the contents of the house.

My sister and I

I was eleven, Vera was eight and it was decided that we should go to stay with our grandparents at Little Barrow for a week during the move. Father took us to our train at Knutsford, and grandfather Mapes met us at Barrow station.

The farm was only a short distance from the station and there was a warm welcome from grandma, who was very special. This was the first time that Vera and I had been away from home without our parents and as we travelled on the train, and on that first night away, I looked after her. We were both anxious to see our new home and also to get back to the family, so the day after they had moved in, we too moved in, going from Barrow to Mouldsworth on the train, just one stop away.

Our new home

Mother had given us careful instructions how to get from Mouldsworth station to the New Pale. It felt like miles to us, but then, at last, we arrived at the corner where we got our first sight of our new home. It was most impressive, standing on its own on the hill. We ran the rest of the way and mother was there to greet us. We were very excited as we started looking round the house. It was so big, with at least seven bedrooms, plus several other rooms upstairs, including the bathroom, and cheese room, and one that later became our billiard room. Mother had sorted out where we had to sleep - Wilfred and I were to be together, Vera had her own room above mother's and father's and Walter and Herbert shared the room opposite hers.

Although there were bedrooms for each of us, I don't suppose that there was furniture for six rooms. Our first thought was what a great place to play hide and seek.

A man trap

As we were exploring the house we found in a bottom cupboard a most peculiar looking object, which looked like a giant rat trap. In fact it turned out to be a man trap. It was a ghastly weapon and it had been used in the past to catch poachers in the forest. I think that it eventually ended up in the museum in Chester.

There were so many things to do that we were all kept busy. All day someone was asking "Do you know where this is?", "Has anyone seen that?". Then someone asked, "Has any one seen the cats?" These were the farm yard cats that didn't come into the house. No one had and some time afterwards we had news from the threshing machine man who said that when he came to move his machine from Long Lane, he discovered two cats in the threshing machine box. I think that we got them back later on.

The good neighbours

While we were having our tea that first day we had a visitor - a lady who was to become a most wonderful friend and who was to have a great influence on my life. Her name was Elsie Priest. She was the wife of an architect, Arthur Priest, and both were key workers at Mouldsworth Chapel. She had brought a dozen cakes that she had baked and a bunch of flowers from her garden. She gave us all a warm welcome and an invitation to Mouldsworth Chapel. All seven of us went the following Sunday and the chapel became a spiritual home for our family - for father and mother until they died, and for the rest of us until we moved away. Herbert and his wife, Ruth, whom he married in 1949, continued to worship there until it closed in 1997.

In those early days when there was no TV and not all the modern means of travel, the local chapel, for us at any rate, was the very centre of our social life. We went every Sunday, often twice, and once or twice during the week.

Mouldsworth Chapel

Slater's Chronicles

A few years ago I was given several old books, including one called 'Slater's Chronicles'. At the time I was not very excited about any of them, for they looked rather dull and uninteresting. However, one day I was getting rid of some books and decided not to give this one away until I had found what it was about. I'm so very glad that I did. I discovered that it was published in 1881, and that the author was a Mr George Slater, a farmer who was born at Gawsworth, not far from Over Peover.

The subtitle was 'Lives and religion in Cheshire'. Mouldsworth Chapel was mentioned - when it was built, and the prime movers of its building - and also information about the New Pale was given.

The New Pale: Place Of Worship.

He writes:

> *"At that time the New Pale, a large farm on the borders of Delamere Forest, was honoured by it being the residence of Mr George Pugh. . . he was not only a Christian man, but it is said that he did more than his predecessors to reclaim and cultivate that large farm. Mr Janion and Mr Pugh worked together for God. . . In the year 1800 Mr Janion was living at Mouldsworth, Here a chapel was erected in the year 1815. Methodism had obtained a footing, and the chapel has continued to exist down to the present time (1890)".*

Mr George Pugh, who lived at the New Pale, opened his home for religious services and it appears that these continued for several years. It was a great

Father and grandfather in the turnip field

centre and it was common for devoted men from many parts of the country and even from Manchester to attend Love Feasts and Revival services at the New Pale. A Love Feast was a simple service, in some ways similar to Holy Communion. This all happened in what became our dining room at the New Pale and I never knew about it until reading Slater's Chronicles.

H. Challoner and Sons

My brother Herbert's son David, his wife Janet and their four children, now live at the New Pale, and Herbert, still (in 1997) goes to the farm most days. David's brother Robert with his wife Jane and their two boys live at the next farm, Rangeway Bank. He and David with their father, farm both farms and another one at Tarvin (where Herbert and Ruth live) under the company name of 'H. Challoner and Sons'.

Chester City and County School.

We arrived at the New Pale in the middle of February, just half way through the school term, and in order to gain a place in the school I had to take an entrance exam. I was nervous about this but the headmaster soon put me at ease. He just asked me one or two questions about myself, my interests, my home and then left me to do the exam. After looking at what I had written he told me that he would be happy to offer me a place in the school and that I could start the following Monday. It wasn't easy starting in the middle of a school year and also in the middle of a term.

My non-academic career

Looking back on my academic career, I realise that there are a number of factors that didn't help me. I mentioned in the last chapter that, before I was eleven, I had missed over two years schooling and then when I gained a place in the City and County school, I soon discovered that living as I did out in the country, gave the city boys a big advantage over me. I had to leave home in the morning soon after eight to catch my train at Mouldsworth. It was not a fast train, in fact its critics used to say that the Cheshire Lines railway was the only railway in the country that was mentioned in the Bible for there we read, in the very first chapter, that "God created all creeping things. . ." It did seem at times to creep and took the best part of half an hour to get to Chester Northgate station. Then I had another one and a half miles to walk to Handbridge to the school. Every morning I arrived twenty minutes late and had to stand in the corridor along with other late comers and any Roman Catholics who were excused Protestant prayers. We had to go on Saturday mornings and, although school finished at noon, it was half past one before I got home; and on Wednesday, which again was supposed to be a half day, I didn't get home until 3.40. My best friend at school, Charles Tremlett, was a city boy and always came top of the form. Charles would be home, have his meal, do his homework and be out playing before I got home.

Tremlett cartridges

Sometimes, instead of coming home on Friday or Saturday, I would stay in Chester with Charles. His mother was very kind to me, just like a second mother. His father was headmaster of Love Street School for Boys. Charles loved to come to stay at the New Pale. We could both write many pages about the things that we did. I want now to describe just one of those things.

I earned my pocket money helping to keep the rabbits from taking over. In those days it was always a big battle. A mother rabbit might have as many as five or six young ones in a litter and these could themselves start breeding in about six months. Each doe had more than one litter a year so the rabbit population increased rapidly and needed to be culled, or the farm would become one huge rabbit warren.

I used quite a lot of cartridges, and these were expensive, and took a good percentage of my pocket money, so when Charles suggested that, if I saved my empty cartridge cases, he would refill them, I thought it a good idea. I soon collected a number of empty cases and he collected the other things necessary. For each cartridge we required:

1. A detonating cap.
2. Two pieces of felt about the size of a trouser button.
3. Ingredients for making gunpowder.
4. Lead for the shot pellets.

We arranged for Charles to come to stay for a weekend when father and mother were away all Saturday. He brought everything with him and we had no time to waste for although he had all that was necessary for the job, the gunpowder and the lead pellets had to be made.

Our own "Shot Tower"

We started by making the lead pellets. This turned out to be a much more difficult job than we expected, but Charles was confident. In Chester there was a tall shot tower where they made lead pellets and he had studied the process. It seemed quite straight forward in theory. All that you had to do was to pour molten lead from a tall building into a tank of cold water. It makes me tremble as I think of it now, and yet then it was just a great challenge and with Charles and all his 'know how', we couldn't go wrong! Or could we?

How to get rid of a tadpole's tail!

We took one of mother's washing tubs to the front of the house, below Vera's bedroom window (which was three storeys up) and filled it with water. I managed to find an old iron saucepan to melt the lead in and a blow lamp to heat it. The strategy was that Charles would melt the lead then I would run upstairs with it to Vera's bedroom, pour this molten liquid down in a very fine stream, so that it formed droplets before reaching the cold water and these would then turn into pellets. That was the theory!

The lead was liquefied. I raced up the stairs with it and quickly began pouring a thin stream of it through the window. It fell straight down into the dolly tub. I then raced down stairs to find Charles almost head first in the tub trying to fish out these little lead pellets. 'Fish out' seemed to be an appropriate description, for in fact what he did bring out were some little bits of lead that looked more like tadpoles than pellets. They each had a tail. Charles decided that if we could get a few feet higher it would just about eliminate their little tails, and this might be achieved if, instead of leaning through the window and holding my arm down, I should stand on something in the bedroom and pour; holding my arm up. In theory that sounds possible, but in practice it was very difficult.

However I could see that this was what was needed, so, again with the molten liquid, I ran upstairs, stood on a chair, held the pan as high as I could and poured. Having poured enough I ran down stairs to find Charles still with his head in the tub pulling out one by one these little bits of lead. They still had tails, but the tails were definitely shorter.

Climbing to success

We decided if only we could get another three feet higher we would just about win. Well, no way was I going up on the roof, but under the barn we had two long ladders which, when clipped together, could double their height and enable me to reach above the window.

Eric and Sheila re-visiting the New Pale. The window at the top right was the scene of the lead shot experiment.

With great difficulty we raised these ladders and with molten lead in my pan I climbed up. Now climbing up a steep double ladder with a pan of molten lead is very difficult and dangerous, but up I went, poured it down, and I was surprised when I reached the ground that I had managed to do it. What is more, although we had not eliminated their little tails altogether they were now short enough to file off. This we did.

Another Gunpowder Plot

Having made the pellets we turned our thoughts to making the gunpowder. Charles had carefully filled three jam jars with the three basic ingredients-charcoal, saltpetre and sulphur. It was now simply a case of carefully weighing the separate amounts out. Although we were only attempting to make one cartridge on this occasion, we did plan to make more for which we would need more gunpowder. He asked for a strong flat tin - having assured me that when we had finished the job it would all wash off. I borrowed one of mother's roasting tins and a wooden baking spoon to stir with. I also got her scales from the pantry. Charles carefully weighed the stuff out and mixed it together. Then he had to add a small amount of water. What a black sticky mess it was. He had to be so careful not to add too much water for before he could use it, it had to be dried into a powder. Now this was not very easy. Charles said it required a *'low continuous heat for about ten hours'*.

A rude awakening

The only suggestion that I had was the oven at the side of the coal fire, where father each night put the sticks with which he lit the fire each morning. It kept warm all night, even after the fire had gone out, and Charles thought it would be ideal. But before he went to bed father would be putting his sticks in it. This meant that we had to wait till he had done this, then I crept down and carefully slipped the roasting tin and its contents amongst the sticks, then went back to bed. Father would be getting up on Sunday morning about seven, so I set my alarm for six thirty.

Just why I didn't hear it go off I don't know, but what I did hear at seven was father from the bottom of the stairs shouting "Eric, what is this black mess in your mother's roasting tin?". I did not attempt to give him an answer from my bed, but rushed down, picked up the tin of gun powder and explained that it was a chemical substance that Charles had made as part of an experiment- which was true, but not the whole truth. Phew! I suppose if father had stuck a match and a spark had made contact with that powder this would have been a different story- if there was a story!

Having got all the parts and the ingredients it was now just a matter of putting them together in the cartridge case. We chose to do this in the room above the dairy. Charles was very careful and I must add very skilful in the way he did this job.

First of all he put in the small ignition cap having carefully removed the old one, then just the right amount of gunpowder, then the first round disc of felt separating the shot from the powder, then the shot, another disc of felt and finally the disc of cardboard that fitted tightly and kept every thing in.

All this was done before Sunday dinner. It was fortunate that mother had more than one roasting tin.

The mushroom cloud

Charles, in a recent letter, takes up the story from his point of view and describes what happened next. Having loaded the gun with the precious cartridge . . . *'We tied it with binder twine to the side of a lorry which was in the drive, and then another long piece of the twine to the trigger'*. (This was in case it blew the gun to pieces!)*' On firing there was a heavy dull thud, followed by a great jet of white smoke mushrooming out to about ten feet in diameter. Meanwhile we could hear the shot pitter pattering along the hedge as it struggled to escape the smoke and reach the road. We just fell about laughing, it was so ludicrous'*.

I am afraid my laughing was cut short, for, when I opened the gun and looked down the barrels I was shocked to see that one of them, instead of it being bright and clean, looked as though it had been painted with tar. I knew that father would be very angry if he saw it like this, and probably Charles would be banned from the New Pale.

Just what could we do? First of all I made a 'pull through' from a piece of rag and a strong cord. Then I dipped the rag in petrol and managed to clean it with this until it shone like the other barrel. I am very glad to say that father never discovered what had happened to his gun, which I think is still used today by one of my nephews.

By the way, that was the first cartridge that Charles and I made - *and the last!*

A holiday adventure in Scotland

Mr Ramshaw was our history master in the fourth form; he was short and fat with very red cheeks and a fiery temper. He was a good teacher and taught one of my favourite subjects. He was a Scot - a Glaswegian - and a keen supporter of Rangers. Whenever they lost on a Saturday it seemed that there was a cloud over the history lesson on Monday. Fortunately for us they did not often lose.

I best remember him for the eight days holiday that he arranged for us in his own native country. This holiday included three days in Glasgow and five days camping at Lochgoilhead. He was proud of his native city. He told us that it was Scotland's leading commercial centre and that the world's most skilful shipbuilders worked in the Clyde shipyards. The ship that was later named "The Queen Mary" was actually being built when we were there. Years later they also built the Queen Elizabeth. He took us round the ancient cathedral and several art galleries and museums.

Rangers

The highlight for me was our visit to the Rangers football ground. I have a feeling that Mr Ramshaw had some official status in the club for we got VIP treatment and the officials who met us all seemed to know him personally. Their stadium impressed us. He told us that it was one of the most modern in the UK and that the facilities for the players were second to none.

A day that I will never forget.

Leaving the YMCA on Monday morning we went by coach to our camp at Lochgoilhead where we had - for the most part - freedom to do our own thing, especially for the first two days. We were all so tired we were glad to lie in the sun and play in the river. It was this playing in the river that nearly led to my departing this life.

What happened was this. Ted Greenway (another of my school friends) and I went off on our own exploring this river. We had our swimming trunks on and for much of the time just paddled. It was never very deep, except for an occasional pool. Although it was a hot day these pools were very cold.

We came to one pool much deeper and wider than the rest. Ted, who was a strong swimmer jumped in and swam straight across. I struggled to cross with my 'dog paddle' style but when I got to the middle I suddenly got a severe cramp. Never had I experienced anything like this before. It felt as though powerful cold arms came up from the depths and held me in a tight grip. I was completely helpless and quickly sank. I yelled as hard as I could for Ted then sank again, and when I came up I was desperate and in a dangerous situation.

Ted heard me at last, came rushing back, jumped in and swam towards me. As he got near I tried to grab him, but he managed to punch me away and, getting hold of my hair, he pulled me to the side. I was never so glad in my life to have my hair pulled and to feel the rocky bottom of the river bed. He helped me on to the bank. By this time he was exhausted and I was in a state of shock. I have always believed that Ted saved my life that afternoon. I'm so thankful that, not only was he a powerful swimmer, but that he had been trained in life saving. Since that experience I've never been happy in any water when out of my depth and have never become a good swimmer.

Ted and I became firm friends, and our friendship continued after we left school. He often came to the New Pale and I often went to Ashley House in Frodsham, where his father was a vet. Ted later followed in his father's footsteps. I have happy memories of that period of my life and could tell many stories about Ted.

Tales of an "Old Banger"

Two stories involved Ted when he was driving a car.

The first was when he was taking his father to a farm. As they travelled along the Frodsham-Helsby road Ted suddenly announced "Dad, look, the steering wheel has come off". Unfortunately it had. But although they ran into the hedge, they weren't hurt, only shocked and shaken.

On another occasion I was involved. Ted bought an old Riley car. He loved to drive it fast and I must confess he scared me at times . . . and enjoyed doing this.

He would drive close up to the rear of a big lorry and then swerve round it. On one occasion I thought we would have gone under this particular vehicle and automatically pressed hard on the floor boards as though I was applying the brake. There was a horrible crunching sound and my foot went right through the panel. Ted was not happy with me.

CHAPTER FOUR

FARMING IN THE THIRTIES

Summer and winter, and spring time and harvest,
Sun, moon and stars in their courses above,
Join with all nature in manifold witness
To thy great faithfulness, mercy and love.
Thomas O. Chisholme.

In the early 1930's I was still at school but Wilfred, Walter and Herbert were at home working on the farm. It was in the days when a lot of labour was needed. Most of the labour-saving machines had not been invented, or at least we hadn't got them at the New Pale. Milking was done by hand. There was no silage and the grass was cut with a mowing machine pulled by a team of horses.

The corn harvest

There were no combine harvesters then. A team of horses would pull the binder but before they started, men with scythes would cut their way into the field then cut right round the edge of the corn to stop the horses trampling it all down. The corn was put into bundles, tied by machine then thrown out in long rows round

the field. Every sheaf had to be picked up and put into stooks, each stook having eight sheaves. If the sheaves got wet the stooks had to be pulled apart, each sheaf put on its head and the bottom or butt end opened out to help it dry. Then it was carted off and stacked in the barn. After a long day - for we kept on until sunset - we would be ready for a good supper, often of poached eggs on toast. An army of men was needed on a big farm for all these many jobs. This was not the end of the operation. The big job on the farm in winter was threshing. For several days a mighty steam engine, a huge threshing box and baler with a team of men, would be engaged in threshing all these sheaves of corn. Today that whole operation-the cutting, threshing and carting-is done in one day by a combine harvester and about three men.

Reaseheath Agricultural College

Father was anxious for us all to get the best training and in spite of the fact that money was never plentiful in those days; he managed to send Wilfred, Walter and Herbert to fee paying schools. Then he wanted to send us all to Reaseheath Agricultural College but because of the expense and manpower shortage, Wilfred missed out on this. The rest of us went, Walter in 1931, Herbert in 1933 and I went in 1935.

Eric with some fellow students at Reaseheath College.

Reaseheath Agricultural College

I asked Herbert to write down a few memories.

Herbert's memories of Reaseheath

"Mr Mercer was the principal, and very highly respected by the staff and students. He gave long lectures on farming, past and present. He seemed always to wear plus fours, and wherever he went his two lovely cocker spaniel dogs went with him.

Mr Carr, the vice-principal, was a Scot, a good man, the son of a farmer, whose father and brothers farmed near Aberdeen. I still remember some of the stories that he told of fattening cattle on neeps (turnips) with straw bedding up to their bellies. I sent him a letter on his 100th birthday.

Other staff included Mr Hankinson, animal husbandry, Mr Barratt and Mr Shewell Cooper, horticulture. The farm manager was Mr Jackson. The female staff, Miss Bennion and Miss Black were in charge of the dairy section, specialising in cheese making. Students were taught how to make really good cheese, and to scrub and keep the dairy utensils scrupulously clean".

The miracle of just one grain of wheat

Herbert said that he still remembered some of the lectures that Mr Carr gave. I'll never forget one such lecture, for I've referred to it in many Harvest festival services, illustrating the wonderful plan God has made to feed ALL the world. He had prepared his lecture well. On the blackboard was a map of the world; in his hand was one little grain of wheat. "I hold in my hand a miracle of creation" he said. "If you took this grain of wheat and sowed it, it could produce at least twenty grains. If you then sowed those twenty grains you would get twenty times twenty. Those four

47

Eric (front centre) and fellow students from Reaseheath

hundred would produce eight thousand and so on. In ten years time from that one little grain you could get enough corn to feed every man woman and child in the world. Unbelievable but true".

God's wonderful plan to feed the world

Moreover there are more than fifteen thousand different strains of wheat so that if it is the right strain, wheat can be grown even in the Equatorial region and on the Himalayan slopes. If that is not enough, it is a fact that every single month of the year there is a harvest of wheat being gathered somewhere in the world.

God's harvest calendar

I mentioned that on the blackboard there was a large map of the world giving a list of wheat harvests. I kept a record of that lecture and of the harvest calendar.

There is a wheat harvest in: January in Argentina, February in India, March in Egypt, April in Persia and Mexico, May in Central Asia, June in America and France, July in S. Russia, August in Germany and England, September in Scotland and Serbia, October in Scandinavia and Finland, November in S. Africa, December in Australia.

God made the promise that as long as the earth remains seed-time and harvest will not fail. Although there have been harvest failures in different parts of the world, there has never been a year when all the harvests have failed, and if only those who have more than enough would share with those without, then in a very short period of time poverty and starvation would be no more.

The General Farm Course

Walter, Herbert and I all took the General Farm Course. It lasted for one year and was both practical and theoretical.

There was animal husbandry which included learning the names of the many different breeds of sheep and pigs and cattle. I especially enjoyed the lectures given by the visiting vet and was very pleased when I came top in one of his exams. We had a skeleton of a horse, and had to remember the names of its different bones, we also had a big picture of the inside of a cow, showing its different stomachs and had to write an essay entitled 'From Grass to Milk'. That was a fascinating study. The cow doesn't bite the grass, but pulls it up with her tongue. She then swallows it into her first stomach where it is mixed with powerful digestive juices; after a while she regurgitates this half digested food in small quantities into her mouth. This is her cud, and some time after cows have grazed, they will lie down and, looking very content, will chew their cud, then swallow it into their second stomach, and bring up more cud, and so the cycle goes on. At the end of this process a barrow full of grass, can go in through one entrance and come out as milk through four little taps conveniently placed at the other end. Fantastic.

Where are you going with that milk?

The practical side of the course included many things, such as learning how to milk. Some of the students had very little experience of farming, and had certainly never milked a cow. After milking my first cow at Reaseheath I was taking the milk up to the dairy, when the farm foreman shouted, "And where do you think you are going?" I told him that I was going to the dairy. "You have never finished milking that cow, I'm sure", he said and went and felt her udder. I told him that I began milking when I was twelve.

The tup with the red belly

One of the things that a young farmer has to do is learn all about the reproductive processes. If, for instance, a ewe is to have a lamb she must be put to a tup, (male sheep). Each tup's belly would be painted with special paint, one red and the other blue. They would then be turned loose among the ewes during the mating season. The ewes served by red belly will have red on their backs, and the others will have blue. Those with no colour will either be left longer with the red and blue team, or taken to another tup who 'might do better'.

A man "worth his weight in gold"

With cattle it is very important to know the date that a heifer is going to calve, for she does not give any milk until she has had a calf and a farmer tries to prevent his milk production levels from varying too much. In order to do this he needs to work out just at what particular time he wants the heifer to come into milk production and having done this he needs to know when to put this heifer to the bull to be served, when she is on heat. This is when a good cowman who is very observant is worth his weight in gold. If he misses just one time, that means a months delay in having a calf, which means the loss of a whole month's milk from that heifer. With a big herd we might be talking of hundreds of pounds loss. That's why I say a good cowman is "worth his weight in gold". Today many farmers do not keep a bull, but rely on artificial insemination (AI).

Russian Roulette - but it wasn't a game

During the lunch break on the afternoon of the 25th January 1937 one of the day students had been in the wood near the lake having gun practice with a .45 revolver that he had brought from home. It belonged to his father who was a retired army officer. The bell calling us to lectures sounded, so he emptied the gun (it held five bullets), put it in his pocket and came into the lecture. While we were waiting for the lecturer he pulled the gun out and held it to the back of the neck of the fellow in front of him and pulled the trigger. It wade quite a loud click. He then told a girl standing by the black board to "stick 'em up" and clicked again. He then swung it in a circular movement, clicking. With the final click there was a very loud bang and the fellow holding the gun dropped it on the floor clutching his leg which was streaming with blood. A bullet had entered his leg below the knee, and had gone right down to his ankle breaking his ankle bones.

There was a deathly silence in the class room as we all realised what might have happened. Folk came rushing in, an ambulance was called and the man who was in great pain was taken to hospital. There were no more lectures that day, and one or two of the students had to have treatment for shock. I never saw that student or his gun again.

The ref. who swallowed his whistle

Another incident, very funny to many of us, but certainly less dramatic than the one with the gun, resulted in the referee of a football match going into hospital. It was a match between ourselves. A fellow who neither wanted the job, nor knew the rules was recruited as referee, but he didn't have a whistle.

Eventually one was found. It was flat, had a hole through it and one could suck or blow to make it whistle, but to get a good loud sound you had to do a big blow (or suck). Fortunately he did not have to use his whistle much. However on the very last kick of the match a goal was scored. He came running up with his whistle in his mouth, but he sucked and swallowed it. He was jumping up and down, but so were the rest of us and it was a while before he could let us know that he had swallowed his whistle.

Every time he took a deep breath he whistled. Some of us laughed - it was hard not to. He tried to tell us off, shouting "It's not funny" and whistling as he did. One of the staff took him to the local hospital in Nantwich. After discovering that it was a flat smooth whistle, the doctor sent him out saying "Now if you get any severe pain you must come back at once, but I think it should pass through without any serious problem". It did, but he never acted as ref. again. Less kind students would sometimes shout "Where's your whistle, ref.?"

This incident took place near the end of term when we were taking exams, and after seeing the questions in one paper, he conveniently developed a 'whistle pain', and missed the exam!

Back home on the farm

The year at Reaseheath seemed to go quickly, for I had enjoyed it so much more than I did my school days in Chester. The reason was I was interested in every subject, and it had relevance for me. Whilst I knew more than most about the practical side of farming, I knew less about the theory. I enjoyed the instructions that we were given by an expert hedge layer. In those days we took great pride in a well layed hedge and a ploughed field of perfect furrows. Today the main concern is in getting the job done as quickly as possible.

Smiler and Boxer my good friends

When I first left school all our ploughing was done with single furrow ploughs pulled by teams of horses in pairs. We had five horses at that time - Blossom, Flower, Punch, Smiler and Boxer, which meant we could have two teams ploughing, and this would occupy most of autumn and winter. I well remember the very first field that I ploughed on my own with my own team, Smiler and Boxer. I loved those horses. They were quite different characters, Smiler was so cheerful and such a willing worker. She would work until she dropped. Boxer was the stronger of the two, but a bit clumsy and needed a much stronger pull on the rein, especially when turning round on the headland.

Getting ready for the job

I didn't find it easy to get up at six in the morning, especially on a dark, cold winter's day. However it was good to go down the yard to the stable and be greeted by Smiler. She would give a little 'whinny' and throw her head about and give a swish of her tail. Walter Worrall was our head waggoner. He'd been at the farm long before we came, and he too loved his horses and was proud of them. We would give them a bowl of corn to begin with and then clean out the wet and dirty straw, before giving them a good combing and brushing. Then came the business of putting their harness on. This varied according to the work they had to do.

A plough similar to those which Eric would have used

When the horses were yoked up, we went for our breakfast, which usually consisted of porridge, bacon and egg, and toast and marmalade. Mother would always give me a flask of Ovaltine, and a good slice of home made fruit cake for my 'baggin' (mid-morning snack) which I would have about ten thirty. The discipline of getting up early every morning as a farmer has been good for me, and I've continued to do so throughout my ministry.

A young man with his hand to the plough

The first field that I ploughed was twenty two acres. It was important that the first furrow should be straight so father drove the horses for this one and then I took over, using the furrow father cut as a guide. A pair of horses and a single furrow plough could plough about one and half acres each day. I suppose it took me about three weeks to finish my first field. It was hard work, and I must have walked many miles altogether, but father said that I'd done a good job and this gave me great satisfaction.

On Robin red breast's territory

During the ploughing of this field I found a friend. It was a little robin. Each cock robin has its own territory and I was on his territory. He didn't follow me up the field but waited at the headland near the road until we came round. When I had my 'baggin' he came to me and I began taking him a piece of bread, and tried to get him to eat out of my hand. He never did but he sat on the toe of my boot one day. I'm sure that he recognised me, for when I went  on my bicycle to see my friends the Greenways at Frodsham and passed this field I would call and he would come to me.

The business of milking

At that time we had over sixty cows, and these had to be milked twice a day, starting at six each morning, and again at four o'clock in the afternoon. All

52

workers on the farm had to learn how to milk, and all took their turn at it. Usually there would be about six or seven of us at each milking session, which meant we would have an average of ten cows each to milk. It was quite a pleasant job, especially in winter, when it was cold outside, but warm in the shippon as sixty cows produce quite a lot of heat. It was hard work, but I enjoyed it.

The minister helps with the milking

My ability to milk came in useful later when I became a minister. On two occasions at least I was called in to help a farmer in real need.

The first was at Aston. Mr Cox, a steward at the church there, had a small holding with seven cows, which he milked by hand. He had a bad accident to his hand while hedge cutting and was sent at once into the hospital at Crewe. His daughter, Joyce, came to the manse in great distress. Since leaving her dad in hospital she had tried to get someone to milk, but had failed, and asked if I could help. I did, and continued to help for about six weeks, sharing the work with a retired farmer.

I have trouble with Maggie

The second time was thirty five years later, after I had retired. The farmer was Wilf Edgerton and he too was a steward in the local church, at Hassall Road, Alsager. He had thirty six cows and milked by machine. He was ill and needed to go into hospital for treatment. I offered to help him, but he warned me that I might have trouble with Maggie (he knew all his cows by name). She behaved herself  with him, but she didn't like the vet and would kick at him if he came near her. I knew that if I couldn't milk Maggie, I couldn't milk any for she would have to be milked. So I spent some time watching Wilf and trying to get to know her.

Barbara Woodhouse to the rescue

At that time a Mrs Barbara Woodhouse had become famous for the way she was able, not only to train dogs, but tame wild horses. The secret was that she was gentle and very patient with them, and slowly got into a position where she would be able to breathe into their nostrils. Once she had done this for a short time, she found it bonded her to the animal, and she was able then to tame and train the wildest of horses.

I decided to try Barbara's method on Maggie. When Wilf finished milking her, I took her some more cow corn, stood by her, and began to stroke her. She began to sweat and was frightened, and I was frightened too which made matters worse. It was essential that we both had to accept each other. I hadn't seen Maggie kick, but I knew from experience that a cow can have a very vicious and violent kick, and as the milker stands at her rear ready to put the machine on her he is in a very vulnerable position.

Bonding with Maggie

I came a number of times to get used to the machine and the cows and, gradually, I felt Maggie was beginning to accept me. I managed to stroke her neck, and behind her ears, and got into a position where I could breathe gently up her nose. It was not easy, but she allowed me to do it. I then told Wilf that I would have a go the next day. I gave her a generous helping of cow corn and gently washed her udder with warm water. She kept turning and looking at me, but had lost her fear. All this time I was quietly praying as I leaned on her and put on the teat cups. I stood back with a great sigh of relief as she was milked. I had managed to bond with Maggie so Wilf was able to go into hospital, and I was able to do his milking. When you bring in your pint of milk, think not only of the milkman who delivered it, but also the milkman who milked.

The champion milker.

I suppose that of the four of us, Walter was the most skilled, especially when it came to hand milking. There was often real competition between the milkers to see who could milk the fastest. This was where Walter showed that he was far better than any of us, and is why father suggested that he enter for the milking competition held annually at the Cheshire County Show. This was a big event, and farmers' sons and daughters from all over the county took part.

I wasn't able to go to the show to see Walter compete but had to wait at home for news of the result, knowing that he would be one amongst many competitors, and this was his first attempt. Imagine our surprise and delight when Walter came in proudly carrying the certificate showing that he had won first prize! This meant that he had qualified to milk in the North of England trials in Stafford. If he came first, second or third it meant he would qualify to milk at the London Dairy Show open to competitors from all over the UK. He went to Stafford and gained a second there, so qualified for London. There he gained third prize. We were all very proud of him. Milking was only one of the things around the farm that he excelled in, for he won a prize for ploughing and also for hedge laying.

Hockenhull Hall.

Walter was ambitious and enterprising. Someone who knew father said "he's a chip off the old block". He certainly had more of father's characteristics than the rest of us.

When he took his milking can and stool to Chester Show that day, it was a brave thing to do for he faced very strong competition. But he was determined, and put everything into the effort. This determination and effort enabled him to prove that he was one of the best young milkers in the country. Whilst still in his early twenties his thoughts began to turn towards having a farm of his own.

At that time he had met a young lady who, like him, had been a student at Reaseheath. Her name was Edna Stretch and her father had a fine herd of Jersey

Hockenhull Hall

cattle. Like Walter, Edna was very gifted in many ways. She played the organ in the local church at Helsby; she won prizes at the Cheshire Show in the Country Crafts section. Like Walter, she was ambitious and, like him, ready to accept a challenge, a characteristic that she would need in the days that lay ahead. They began looking seriously for a place of their own. When it was announced that Hockenhull Hall, Tarvin, was coming on the market, no one thought for a moment that Walter would be interested. It was over two hundred acres, and the house itself was more like a stately mansion than a farm house, even bigger than the New Pale itself.

However, both Walter and Edna were very interested, although it was acknowledged that the upkeep of the house, and the alterations needed to bring the shippons and other buildings up to the standard required for a modern farm would need much hard work and great expense. Mother was more hesitant. She felt that the farm was too big for Walter to manage and the house far too big for a young bride not yet twenty-one with her husband just twenty three. However Father saw great potential in the farm. His verdict on the soil was that it was very good and with the right management would produce some excellent crops. In this he was proved right.

The sale was by public auction. There was a lot of interest from farmers all over the country, but the huge house was a stumbling block to many. When I came home from school that day, I rode from the station on my bicycle faster than usual, anxious to hear how they had gone on and hoping that they had bought it, for it would mean that Walter and Edna would be living quite near. Walter was just coming out of the shippon when I went rushing down the drive and one look at his face told me all I wanted to know.

There was of course a tremendous lot to be done when the purchase was made. We all rallied round. Father lent men and machines, and Herbert spent a lot of time there helping. When I was on holiday from school, I almost lived there and counted the days when I would be able to leave school and join the team.

A foolish decision

I was sixteen on 27th February 1934, the year the farm was bought and technically was old enough to leave school. Whilst I was very keen to leave it was a foregone conclusion that I would take my exams first. I ought to have spent that Easter break studying; in fact I spent all of it at Hockenhull with Walter, working hard and enjoying it. One day he said to me, "I do wish that you didn't have to go back to school" and I began to question the need to go back. My job was secure and the exams had no real significance from that point of view.

It was on Easter Sunday (April 1st that year!) in the evening after we had all been to chapel that I plucked up the courage to talk to father about it. His reply was "I think you'd be very foolish not to go back, but it's up to you". If it was up to me then my mind was made up, but when I spoke to mother, she was shocked, and said it would be very wrong and that I was letting the school down and would one day regret it. How very right she was, and how very wrong and foolish I was in the end to decide to leave.

I hated going against mother's wishes. It was one of the very few times that I ever did and - if you read on - you will discover that I did have very good reason to regret it. But I loved my work, and it was such a relief to think that I had no more exams to take, no more studying to do, and it was good to be free to continue to help Walter.

A farm transformed

Walter and Edna were married later that year in Helsby Parish Church. After their honeymoon they tackled the mammoth task at Hockenhull Hall together - both inside the house and out on the farm - and in less than three years the place was transformed. All the old shippons and out buildings had been changed and replaced by up to date buildings - including a new dairy. Walter built up an excellent stock of tuberculin tested cattle, modernised the piggeries and filled them with over three hundred pigs. In the house itself they had made many alterations and Edna made good use of the banqueting hall where she hosted lovely parties.

It was at this time that their baby daughter Daphne was born, bringing great joy to her proud parents.

They had many exciting plans for the future, but these were tragically cut short.

The darkest of my life

In November of that year I was taken ill. I had a ruptured diaphragm causing me much pain. On the 8th I had an operation, which was followed by a period of convalescence and on the 25th I went with mother for a week's holiday to Blackpool. The very next day we had an urgent call to come home because Walter was ill - this was on Friday the 26th. On the Sunday the lung specialist came out to Hockenhull but he was helpless to do anything, for the antibiotics which are available today, were not available then. On Monday morning at 11 am Walter died of pneumonia.

That was the darkest moment of my life.

A brother who set us a wonderful example

He was only twenty-six years old, but in those twenty-six years had done more than some men do in sixty years. And, what is more, whilst he was always very busy, he always had time for God and the things of God. He never allowed his work to prevent him from going to church on Sunday, and only a few days before he died he was to have presided at a meeting concerned with the welfare of people who had special needs.

Walter had got his priorities right. That was a lesson that I never forgot and I thank God for him.

His funeral

His funeral was at Tarvin Parish church and this large ancient church was filled with mourners; family and friends, representatives of the Methodist Church, National Farmers Union, Reaseheath Agricultural College, Chester Young Farmers Club and farmers from far and wide. The Chester Chronicle on the following Thursday devoted three columns of the paper to Walter - his life, his achievements, his death and funeral and a full list of mourners and wreaths, and also a photograph.

Walter Thomas Challoner

The account opened with the words "Tarvin and district was shocked this week by the sudden death of a brilliant young farmer in the person of Mr Walter Thomas Challoner, Hockenhull Hall, Tarvin. . . . The respect in which he was held was evidenced by the large attendance at the service which was conducted by the Rev. M. H. Ridgeway and the Rev. L. W. Tattersall."

His death was a tragic loss to us all, but particularly to his young wife, Edna, and to Daphne and Angela, who never knew her father, having been born after he died. How different life would have been for them and for the rest of us had he lived.

CHAPTER FIVE

THE WAR YEARS

*Surely there's a better way to settle disputes
than by destroying the lives of the most promising
young people in the world.*

Bert Bissell.

"Jack, the war has started"

There are certain moments in history that have etched themselves into the memory of generations of people. One such moment was the Sunday morning that Prime Minister Chamberlain declared " We are now at war with Germany". It was September 3rd 1939. Two days before this father, mother, Vera and I set out for Rhyl to have a day with Grandfather Mapes who was on holiday there, and then to bring him to his home at Little Barrow Hall. We took a picnic with us, and father stopped the car overlooking a golf course near Prestatyn. It was a lovely day, mother had packed up an excellent lunch and we sat on the grass eating and watching two golfers having a good game. It was so peaceful.

Then, suddenly that peace was shattered. A woman came running out of the Golf Club, shouting as loudly as she could, "Jack, the war has started, come in now". Jack and his partner gathered their golf things and hurried from the course as though their lives at that moment were being threatened.

We quickly packed up our picnic basket and made our way to Rhyl where we found Grandfather Mapes standing in front of the hotel waiting for us. He had heard the news and was in a very sombre mood. We walked along the sea front with him, then he stopped and looked far out to sea. He remembered well the first World War, 'the war to end wars' and as he looked out he said sadly "I never expected to live to see the day when another war would be started." We didn't stay long in Rhyl. Our one thought was to get home as quickly as we could but first we had to go to Little Barrow to take grandfather home.

The Black Out

Aunt Al. (mother's youngest sister) was waiting for us in a state of real panic. She knew how her husband - our uncle Arthur - had fought and been wounded in the first World War and still carried a piece of shrapnel in his body, which later moved and was the cause of his death.

She was anxious because it was getting dark and we had not got any masks fitted on the headlights of our car. (I later made a set out of two large size fruit tins by cutting slits across the bottom of the tin, then bending back narrow strips to make "hooded lights" so that the glare from the headlights could not be spotted from above. The trouble was we could not see very far with these masked lights.). We left Aunt Al. putting up 'blackout curtains' to prevent any chinks of light being seen.

Germany invades Poland

In my diary for Friday September 1st I recorded "Germany invaded Poland this morning. Towns bombed. General mobilisation in England and France. Ultimatum sent to Hitler. All large towns are being evacuated". All the next day we listened anxiously to the news on the radio - very few people had TV then. Hitler's troops were forcing their way relentlessly across Poland. It was only a year before that Mr Chamberlain had returned from Munich waving a piece of paper that had been signed by Adolph Hitler which promised peace between our two nations. Now that peace had been shattered, and Mr Chamberlain issued an ultimatum - "If the invading troops were not withdrawn by 11 am on Sunday September 3rd. then Great Britain would be at War with Germany". The troops were not withdrawn, so the nation was officially at war.

The Women's Land Army

We at the New Pale were very much involved. A special recruitment drive had been made in all the major towns throughout the country. We were linked with Liverpool, and lots of office girls and shop girls with no experience of farm work at all volunteered. For some it sounded a lovely job, out in the country, away from the bombs etc. They could serve their country and have fun too. They were in for a bit of a shock. A hostel was opened at Mouldsworth and the first batch of raw recruits arrived there. Local farmers who had been registered to train them, had to collect them, put them through their initial tests and to see which were suitable to go forward for training.

Office girls go potato picking

I'll never forget going down for the first batch of twelve and bringing them back on a flat open lorry drawn by a tractor. They were real Liverpudlians, with a Cilla Black accent, and the first job I had was to get them all to sit down. It is so easy to fall off such a lorry and very dangerous too. As we went from Mouldsworth to Manley and on to the potato field they sang loudly all the way "Roll out the barrel" and "Run rabbit run" and other war time songs. They soon stopped singing however as we bumped across the field, for there were no springs on the lorry. I do wish that I could have recorded on camera these girls getting off the lorry in this field, and the faces of our men as they watched them. Some of them

60

were most unsuitably dressed. One girl wore high heeled shoes, and as soon as she jumped off the lorry, her heels dug into the soil and her shoe came off. Other girls had flimsy blouses, and skirts, and no protective clothing if it rained. It was the first batch, and we never did have another like it; in fact, father told me in future not to bring any girl who was not suitably dressed.

Potatoes are grown in drills and, at that time, most were harvested by men with forks which was heavy work. We did however have a machine for digging them out, and scattering them in a row. The potato pickers then worked in twos and were given a measured length. They had wire baskets not unlike those found in supermarkets today and when these were full they were emptied into sacks which were then weighed, tied up and loaded on to the lorry by the men. We had just about got them sorted out and working quite happily, (although most backs were aching) when some very black clouds came over and the one thing that we dreaded happened; we had a thunder storm. In a matter of minutes the whole field became like a quagmire, and the only shelter we had was under the flat lorry. The only protective clothing that we could offer them was a hessian sack each, which of course was wet and not rain-proof at all, but they were glad of them, for in the wet some of the girls' flimsy blouses became transparent!

Training the Land Army

In all fairness to them, I must say these Liverpool girls put a very brave face on things under the circumstances, and as soon as the rain stopped we took them down to the farm buildings, where they had a good rub down, and a warm drink.

This experience certainly sorted out those who were keen enough and tough enough to do farm work. It was essential for them to be suitably clothed for the job. This was not easy, for besides food rationing, there was clothes rationing. But just as uniforms were found for those in the Navy, Army and Air Force, so they were provided for the women's Land Army. It was our job to train them in basic skills and to select a few for specialised training in tractor driving, ploughing etc. I had this job, and worked with three at a time.

Typical clothing for the land army girls.

Ploughing without a plough

I well remember going into a field with three girls, a tractor and a plough. These girls had got used to driving the tractor but now they had to learn how to plough. It wasn't easy. First they had to hitch the tractor to the plough. This needed care because in those days it was done manually, and the driver had to position the tractor exactly right. This particular day we got through the preliminaries; I did a round with two of the girls sitting on the mud guards of the tractor, watching. There was a cord on the plough that the driver had to pull at the end of the furrow. This caused the plough to be lifted up so that the driver could drive round and position the plough in line with the next furrow, then release the cord and off again.

In order to protect the plough from serious damage when a piece of rock was struck - and we had lots of these - a spring hook was fixed on the point where the tractor was hitched to the plough and on impact with rock it released the plough. Now on this occasion one of the girls was going on her first solo run, whilst the rest of us stood and watched. She started off well, holding firmly to the tractor steering wheel, keeping her eye on a straight furrow. We could hardly believe what happened next. The point of the plough hit a rock, and the safety device released the plough and the poor girl, still holding fast to the steering wheel, continued, quite oblivious that she had lost her plough! Well we who were watching stood helpless, and just laughed our heads off. The question was "What would she do when she reached the end of the field?" Keeping her eye in front, she reached behind for the cord, made one or two attempts to reach it and then, for the first time since starting off, she looked round! I suppose it was one of the biggest shocks that she had ever had; so big she forgot to turn and went into the hedge and then the tractor engine stalled. The poor girl cried and was very cross with us for not warning her but we couldn't have warned her for she wouldn't have heard our shouts. I had some difficulty in persuading her to continue. However, she did, and eventually became a most able plough-woman, having

Eric on the tractor

learnt a vital lesson that she never forgot; "Always look straight ahead, but don't forget also to look behind when ploughing with a tractor". Some of these girls were the 'salt of the earth'. They had to work very long hours, for very low pay and in all sorts of adverse weather conditions. They certainly made a vital contribution to the war effort. One of the Land Army songs that they sang when they gave a concert in the local village hall was:

> *"Back to the land, we must all lend a hand,*
> *To the farms and the fields we must go;*
> *There's a job to be done,*
> *Though we can't fire a gun,*
> *We can still do a bit with the hoe".*

Air raids on the farm

Living as we did out in the country on the edge of the Forest of Delamere, one would have thought that we would be relatively safe from bombs and gun fire. In fact it didn't turn out that way. We had three bombs on the farm; one in the orchard, near to the house, and two in the field close by. We also had two huge land mines that came down attached to large silk parachutes; each mine was about the size of three pillar boxes end to end. One landed in the Well field and when it exploded the blast damaged the farm building, shook the house, broke some windows and caused a vacuum to draw the fire up the chimney. It was getting on for midnight when it happened. The sirens had gone and the anti-

Scouts camping at the New Pale. The hollow behind
the tree is where the land mine fell.

aircraft guns were in action not far from the farm. Our cellar made a good air raid shelter and Mother and Vera were down there, but Herbert, myself and cousin Eileen from Rhyl were still in the dining room practising our first aid. She was doing her war service in the hospital at Rhyl and Herbert and I were training for our Red Cross exam the following week. She had come at the right time for she was able to demonstrate the various things that could be done with triangular bandages and the many uses for splints. She not only told us what to do but allowed us to practise on her and when the land mine exploded, Eileen had arms and legs in splints and bandages. Herbert and I made a dash for the shelter - it felt as though the house might come down - and in the confusion poor Eileen was left on the settee, already bandaged up.

We've thought many times since, that if the house had come down, and we had been rescued from the rubble, the rescuers would have thought that somebody had been quick off the mark putting Eileen in splints!

It so happened

One of the bomb experts came the next day to examine the remains of the mine and he told us that if it had exploded as it came down - the whole of the farm house and buildings could have been obliterated. *BUT IT SO HAPPENED* that it landed first; so I am here writing this account...

After this we decided that we would all go down into the cellar when there was an air raid warning; that is, all except father who said "If I'm going to die, I'd rather die in my bed". Then came the night when a plane dropped a stick of bombs on the farm. We heard the plane, and the guns, and we heard very clearly the bombs whistling down over the house; one dropped in the orchard, the other two in a straight line towards the forest. Some windows were smashed but very little structural damage was done. But the funny thing was that father, in his long night shirt, came hurtling down the cellar steps to join us. I think he thought that statistics show that more people die in bed than anywhere else, so he would be better off in the cellar.

Just why were we on the farm targeted? The fact is that we were not; their target was Liverpool. On a clear day the dome of the Liver buildings and the cathedral can be seen across the Mersey from the farm. A ring of anti aircraft guns were placed in strategic positions round the city, as well as a circle of huge barrage balloons with their long trailing wire cables preventing the planes from flying low. We were told that what happened was that these planes got such a hostile reception that they turned back and tried to destroy the anti aircraft guns, one of which was sited on the edge of the farm.

One of the first of "The Few"

Although we had these close 'shaves' we were so very fortunate compared with those in our merchant ships, battle ships, tanks and planes. The New Pale Lodge, which had been built from the two cottages, known as the Pughs houses had been bought by a young man. He and his family were living there when the war began, and he was called up and became a fighter pilot, flying the famous Spitfire. He was one of those engaged in the Battle of Britain, and when he came on leave would walk across the fields and have a friendly chat. At the height of that Battle these men flew some five or six sorties in one day. Each day we would listen to every news bulletin and hear of the number of enemy planes that had been shot down, and how many of our planes were reported missing. One day our good neighbour was one of these young pilots whose plane was missing. He was one of those of whom Prime Minister Winston Churchill made his most famous remark on the 20th August 1940 -

"NEVER IN THE FIELD OF HUMAN CONFLICT WAS SO MUCH OWED BY SO MANY TO SO FEW"

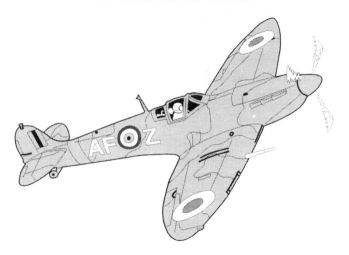

Prisoners of war

Whilst it is true that the Women's Land Army was a great help on the farm, the work for many of them at that time was too heavy. We didn't have the labour saving devices then that they have now. Much of the heavy lifting has been taken out of farming, but then, every sack of potatoes had to be lifted on to a lorry, every sheaf of corn had to be lifted, sometimes as much as ten feet, and heavy bales of straw stacked. It was a man's job.

When Montgomery's famous "Desert Rats" swept across N. Africa, overcoming Rommel's famous tank corps, and capturing thousands of Italian prisoners, it was not only a victory in the deserts of N. Africa but also in the battle for food in this country. This army of prisoners came on to the farms and were a tremendous help. A huge camp was set up on the outskirts of Tarporley, and farmers had to apply to the Commander for the prisoners. At first they would come out in an army truck accompanied by a guard with a gun. As they worked he would watch, but later this was relaxed and they were allowed to come out without any escort. It was one of my jobs to go to collect them.

Father gets his gun

During the whole of the war we only had serious trouble with one of these prisoners. He was from Northern Italy and he had much more in common with the Germans than those from Southern Italy whom he despised. He was sullen and didn't mix with the others, resenting their banter and cheerfulness. He had no intention of working. The job we were doing was carting manure from the midden, and spreading it on the fields. It had to be loaded on the horse drawn carts, but this fellow stood on the midden and hardly lifted a forkful. Father was watching him, and he glared back defiantly It wasn't easy to communicate, for we didn't have an interpreter. When father by gesture made it clear what he must do, he lifted his fork up and threatened father. It was an angry situation. The other prisoners were ready to turn on this fellow and the language was loud and colourful. In the meantime father went in the house, brought out his double-barrelled shot gun and faced this man. I phoned the camp to tell them what had happened. In less than twenty minutes an armed escort arrived. This man was taken back and we never saw him again. The rest of the prisoners were very subdued but worked very hard afterwards.

I must say that I felt very sorry for him. The war had made him regard us as an enemy of his country. In different circumstances we could have been the best of friends. He was just about my own age and I probably would have had much more in common with him than with those from Southern Italy.

Pezzano and Romeo

They came from a land of sunshine and were very home sick. They were not cut out to be fighters and were so glad to have been rescued from the battle field. They were splendid workers and did their very best to please. We became very fond of two of them, Pezzano, and Romeo. We communicated with them by gesture and words that we picked up. I remember Pezzano called me "Erico", father was "Boss", and Herbert was "Sarb". One day I used a word that I had heard them use, and Pezzano said "Erico. No. No. No." and shook his head. I still don't know what I had said or what it meant. I never said it again and I never heard them say it either.

One day Pezzano took me up into the loft above the shippon. He had cleaned it up and during his dinner break, he and Romeo would go and sit there. He made it very clear to me that he would like to sleep up there. Some of the prisoners who could be trusted were allowed to stay out on the farms as long as the farmers could find accommodation and feed them. It was good for us, for it saved us the double journey to Tarporley each day, and it also meant that they could work longer hours so it was a good deal all round. They were happy and so were we.

66

They transformed that loft. We were able to fix them up with tables and chairs, and boxes and they made mattresses out of large hessian sacks which they stuffed. What impressed me most was the way in which they were able to make use of things that we had thrown away. They made a really strong pair of slippers out of a piece of old tyre and an old hessian sack which they pulled to pieces thread by thread. They plaited the threads and somehow wove them together, fastening them to the soles, then they dyed pieces of thread with blackberry juice and stitched a fancy pattern on to each slipper, which they proudly showed to mother.

One day I was ploughing and had a nasty accident, and nearly lost my arm.

When ploughing over rocky ground I hit a rock, put my foot on the clutch, stopped, and pressed hard down on the lever of the plough to lift it above the rock; but my foot slipped off the clutch, the tractor jumped forward, my hand got fast in the lifting lever and I was dragged off the tractor by one arm. *IT SO HAPPENED* that I managed to be pulled clear of the seat or I would have lost my arm. Instead, I tore a number of muscles in my left side and for months was not able to lift much. I tell this story here because Pezzano knew what had happened and made sure that I didn't do anything to strain myself. If he thought I was doing a job that required any lifting, he simply came and took over.

"Erico, war very bad"

It made me want to weep for him, for soon after this our armies had left North Africa and were making their way through the area where all his relatives lived,

Pezzano

around Naples. Towns and villages were being destroyed; civilians as well as soldiers were being killed. I remember finding him weeping one day when bad news had come and all that he could say was, "Erico, Erico, war very bad!"

CHAPTER SIX

FROM PLOUGH TO PULPIT

God does not ask about our ability or inability;
But our availability.

Anon.

One of the questions that I have been asked scores of times is "Why did you leave farming to become a Methodist minister? Weren't you happy on the farm?" I answer that last question with a resounding "*YES*". I enjoyed my work, had a very interesting social life, lots of good friends and was never short of interesting things to do. I was busy with Scouting, my work as Clerk of the Parish Council, teaching in the Sunday School and as a Local Preacher. My hobby was motor bikes and I went several times with Herbert and other friends to the Isle of Man to watch the TT Races. I kept Saturday night free from any meetings and went to the pictures or to Manley Village Hall where at one time I was chairman of the social committee. So life was full and interesting.

And then!

A night that changed my life

 It was a very wet Saturday night and I decided to go to the village hall but discovered that several of my friends were missing and that they had gone to Kelsall where someone by the name of Tom Butler was conducting a Mission. I must say, at that time, missions did not really appeal to me but for want of something better to do, I went. I was wet when I got there and went to the rear of the church into the school room, to take off my wet leggings and motor bike mac. There I met Tom Butler for the first time. He was a very friendly fellow and he made me feel welcome. When I went into the church I was amazed to find it full and it seemed that the majority were young people. When I heard Tom Butler speak, I realised just why so many were there, for I had never heard anyone speak with such conviction and with such a dynamic faith.

That night I was challenged as never before. The next day was a Sunday and my birthday. I always went to Mouldsworth Chapel on Sunday night and when I said I would be going to Kelsall instead, I think my parents suspected that there must be a young lady there who was the attraction! There certainly were several very attractive young ladies there, but that wasn't the real reason why I went. I'd never been faced with such a challenge as on the previous night and felt that God had been speaking to me personally. The challenge was "Are you prepared to go where I want you to go, and to do what I want you to do?"

The big decision

When Christ came face to face with those first disciples long ago, his message was simple and very much to the point "Follow Me". Peter left his fishing and Matthew left the lucrative job of being a tax collector. What was Eric Challoner willing to do? I thought that I was already doing enough. However as we sang the final hymn - one that I had sung many times - for the first time in my life I sang the words and meant them,

> *Just as I am, without one plea,*
> *But that Thy blood was shed for me,*
> *And that Thou bidst me come to Thee,*
> *O Lamb of God, I come.*

That night I did one of the hardest things that I had ever done. I left my seat and, as we sang, I went and knelt at the communion rail. It was so embarrassing, as lots of people knew me, but I knew in my heart of hearts that it was for me the right thing to do that night. Just what it would really mean in the future I had no idea. But I thank God for the decision that was to change my life.

Saturday night was my night - now it is His night

Gradually I began to take more interest in the Bible, not simply as an interesting book to read, but as an instruction and guide book. I carried on with my many activities and went out with the same friends. The problem was that my closest friends had not been to the mission and weren't interested. Then came a big test.

All those who had made a commitment began meeting in what was called the Cliff College Fellowship, every Saturday night. I was invited to join them, but I was quite adamant - Saturday night was "my night out". However the strange thing was that the things that we did became less and less interesting to me. It must have been almost three months after the mission that I decided to go to a Saturday night meeting. I enjoyed it so much. I knew that this was the place for me and these were the folk that I wanted to be with, so from then onwards I joined them every Saturday night.

A taste of real ministry

I kept on with my Scouting, the big difference being that I was not simply anxious for them to pass the various Scouting tests, but put much greater emphasis on what it meant when a Scout promises "to do his duty to God". As a Local Preacher I found a new purpose and a new power in my preaching. It was at this time that I received an invitation to conduct special services at Snelson, the very place that I had attended when a little lad at Long Lane Farm, Over

Peover. It was Youth Sunday, and there were services in the morning, afternoon and evening. Mother, Herbert and Vera came with me and we were all invited to dinner and tea at Newhall, the home of Mr and Mrs John Johnson, Betty, Mary and Dean. I was very nervous about these services and I said so to my old friend Mrs Priest who promised to pray for me. As it was Youth Sunday. I decided to challenge the young people as I had been challenged at Kelsall. When I made an appeal in the afternoon service, several came forward and knelt at the communion rail, the first being Dean Johnson who was then a young chap of thirteen. I can't easily describe my feelings, but I knew that God had been with me and prayers had been answered. Dean was the great-nephew of Foden Dean who had been such a help to my parents.

My call to the ministry

The next morning I was up before six as usual and after milking and breakfast went with the tractor and corn drill to the Well field, which is on the edge of Delamere Forest, and started sowing oats. I had with me on the drill a young fellow whose name was Geoff Lloyd. My mind was very much on what had happened the previous day at Snelson and I became conscious that God was calling me to leave the job I had been trained for, and loved, and to offer for the ministry.

Obstacles in the way of my becoming a minister

For three days I wrestled with this idea quite convinced in my own mind that it was out of the question for me, so I did not say a word to anyone. However, instead of going away, the call became stronger, so on the Wednesday night I went on my motor bike to Kelsall to see the Rev. Percy Robinson, the minister. He was a good friend and had also been a farmer before becoming a minister. I told him of my "call". The thing that surprised me most was the fact that he was not surprised, and seemed to have half expected it. I quickly explained to him just why it was quite out of the question for me to become a minister and spelt out the reasons, one by one.

1. I had previously had serious trouble with my eyes and been to see a Mr Phillips, a well-known eye specialist in Liverpool. My trouble was that, if I did any concentrated reading, I would get a severe pain in one eye. He had prescribed glasses but they were no help, so I did no concentrated reading.
2. I had left school before taking my exams.
3. My responsibility on the farm.

Mr Robinson listened, and said "Eric, if God has called you - and I believe that he has - you must obey that call; take just one step at a time and all those hurdles will be overcome". I had read books where this sort of thing had happened to others, but I had no faith at all that it would happen to me. Mr Robinson then said a prayer. I looked at the clock, and saw it was far later than I had realised, and quickly left for home.

When I arrived home, mother asked, "Is everything all right? You haven't had an accident on that motor bike have you?". I assured her that I hadn't and said that I had been discussing with Mr Robinson the possibility of my becoming a Methodist minister. "You know very well that you couldn't be a minister", she said "but it's too late to discuss it now; go to bed or you wont be up in the morning". I must say that I was very relieved to have told my parents. I would now be able to discuss the matter openly.

The first hurdle

The next morning, up as usual before six, milking, then breakfast with father, mother and Vera. No one mentioned what had been said the night before. I broke the silence by saying "I meant what I said last night about the ministry". Mother replied "Eric, you know very well that Mr Phillips told you that you had a serious problem with one of your eyes, but as long as you don't put any strain on it then you might be all right. To become a minister would mean continuous eye-strain because of all the necessary study. He would be very much against that, if you were to go and see him". I said that I would be happy to go. However, father said I would probably have to wait weeks for an appointment.

I waited till after nine and 'phoned his secretary. *IT SO HAPPENED* that they had a cancellation only a few minutes earlier for an appointment at 11.45 that morning. I could have it if I could get there in time. I said that I could and right away got ready and set off for Liverpool. Rodney Street Liverpool, is a very imposing street; the doors have brass plates giving the name of a specialist or doctor. Mother and I were ushered into the reception room to wait. I was quietly praying that I would have a good report.

Mr Phillips asked if I was having problems so I told him that I was considering changing my job, which would involve me in a lot of concentrated study and I questioned if my eye would stand the strain. He studied my records, examined my eyes and was most surprised to discover a tremendous improvement in my bad eye. He gave me a new prescription for glasses and said that hopefully I would be able to study without any ill effect. I felt like singing the Doxology.

This was hurdle number one behind me. I would add in passing that as I type these words some fifty three years later, my eyes are fine and, apart from tiredness, have not caused me a moments pain or worry in all these years. I could say with the Psalmist, "It is the Lord's doing, and is marvellous in our eyes".

Hurdle number two

The second hurdle was my lack of academic qualifications. I had a full time job on the farm but managed to take time off to study when I could be spared. I got up a bit earlier and studied in my dinner hour also. I had a good ASM (Assistant

Scout Master) in Neville Calvelly who was able and willing to take over much of my scout work and I cut down on some of my other activities.

IT SO HAPPENED that we had at Mouldsworth a Miss Ruth Johnston, who was a school teacher and a Local Preacher. (She eventually married a Methodist minister, Rev. Kenneth Fletcher.) Ruth was a real 'God send' to me. She discussed with Mr Robinson the syllabus of studies that I required, and planned my tuition. I went one evening a week to see her.

Cliff College Mission

IT SO HAPPENED that during this period of intensive study a team of students from Cliff College came to the circuit for a mid-term mission. The Principal of the college, the Rev. J. A. Broadbelt, came over to see them and our minister told him about me and the difficulties I was having studying for the ministry. He came over to the New Pale and told me that if I came to Cliff they would help me to get through the exams. I was thrilled with the idea and father agreed, but said that there might be a problem about my leaving farming for I was in a reserved occupation. I would have to appear before the War Agriculture Executive Committee. This only met once every two months. But, *IT SO HAPPENED* that it was meeting in Crewe the following Friday. The chairman was a friend of the family and arranged - at very short notice - for me to appear before the board. I got my release, but was still not free, for it meant that I was now eligible to be called up into the army.

Now *IT SO HAPPENED* (unknown to me) that the person responsible for sending out the army Call-Up notices had been attending the mission. I was told to give him the papers releasing me from agriculture and on the following Wednesday I received my 'Call-up' papers. The very next day I appeared before the Army Medical Board. But because of the accident that I had on the tractor I failed my medical and so was exempt from army service, and free to go to Cliff. *IT SO HAPPENED* that the following day the students were going back to Cliff in a coach and I went with them!

I still marvel at the remarkable series of 'coincidences' that all happened in such a short space of time. I was reminded of the words spoken by the Rev. Percy Robinson when I went to him first of all. "Eric, if God has called you - and I believe that he has - you must obey that call, taking just one step at a time."

Cliff College

I was very much indebted to my father for enabling me to leave the farm as this created a gap that had to be filled. There were complications but this 'hurdle', (number 3) was also overcome in a remarkable way and as I travelled on the coach with the students to Cliff I kept thinking I was dreaming. It was a dream come true. I very quickly settled down to my new life there and enjoyed the opportunity to study. The Principal told me that all the staff would be willing to help me in my studies and I must use the library and borrow any books that I needed. He also told me that the Rev. George Allen would supervise all my studies for the Candidates exam, and give me any help that I needed. I was greatly helped by his Bible studies.

District Candidates Committee : Chester

I took all the written exams in the front room of his house, at Cliff Park, but the oral exam had to be taken in Chester at the District Candidates committee. At this committee I had to give my "call to preach", and face questions on the books I had read and my knowledge of the Bible. The members of the committee had all my exam results. Some of these I felt were not very good and my book list was poor.

A Bible cricket match

Now the day before this committee, I had a choice of revising all morning for it, or going to Mr Allen's Bible Lecture on the Book of Job. It was much more sensible for me to revise, for I knew there was little chance of my being questioned on Job. But I felt led to go to the lecture. He explained that the book of Job faces the problem of suffering and how in the past it was thought that man's suffering was a penalty for wrong doing. Job was adamant that he was innocent, and his three friends - one by one - tried to prove that he had sinned. Mr Allen opened his lecture with the words "The Book of Job reminds me of a cricket match. Job is batting and his three friends are trying either to bowl him out or catch him out". He then went on to describe their different styles of attack.

I went by train to Chester and took several of the books that were on my list but only had time to look at one of them - "What Methodists Believe and Preach" by Dr. Henry Bett and I studied the chapter headings. The committee was presided over by the Chairman of the District. I was asked to give my "call to the ministry", and was quite happy about this part. Then came the questions. "Mr Challoner, there aren't many books on your list, how do you account for this?" I explained that in addition to having a full time job on the farm, I had been a Scoutmaster, Clerk of the council, and Local Preacher and found little time for extra reading. He then said "You have Dr Bett's book 'What Methodists believe and preach' ; what does he say on this subject?" I recited the chapter headings.

He then questioned me on the Bible and asked if I preferred to read the New Testament or the Old. When I said the New, he replied "But I hope that you do read the Old". I assured him that I did. Now I could hardly believe the next question. *IT SO HAPPENED* that he asked "Does that include the Book of Job?" I said without hesitation and full of confidence that it did. "What are your thoughts on this book?", he asked. I said that it in some ways it reminded me of a cricket match, and was able to remember what Mr Allen had said the day before in his lecture. My answer seemed to impress him and to amuse some members of the committee.

74

Another step forward

I was then asked to leave the room while they reached a decision. There were three other candidates and we had been questioned separately. As we discussed amongst ourselves the questions that we had been asked, I didn't hear one that I could have answered as well as those that I had. When I was called in, the Chairman said that they were going to recommend that my name go forward to the District Synod, which meant that I had got over yet another 'hurdle'. As I travelled back to Cliff, I just thanked God for the way I had been helped, and for the growing confidence that I now had in Him.

Long Preston Mission

It was a great relief for me to get the exams behind me, I was now able to concentrate on the college lectures and other activities which included going out on Team Missions.

In my diary for Saturday March 16th, 1946 I have written, "One of the happiest moments of my college life. Reg Spooner, Jack Aitkin and I were asked to meet in the Principal's study.... He announced that we were each to have the responsibility of leading a Mission....." Each team had six men and mine included my friend Bill Stubbs from Kelsall and we were to go to the Long Preston circuit in Yorkshire.

Cliff students. Eric is at front right.

Eric and Bill Stubbs at Long Preston

Mary and Martha

We were to work in pairs and Bill and I were in Long Preston itself. They had a pastor whose name was Kenneth Snow. This was a memorable experience for all of us and proved to be a most valuable training period for my ministry. We were to stay in the home of two sisters called Metcalf. The very first day we were there, we named them Mary and Martha - for they reminded us so much of the two sisters who entertained Christ during His earthly ministry. Mary was quiet and thoughtful and Martha was always busy. They had a small farm with a few cattle, sheep, pigs and hens and it was Martha who looked after all these. Martha believed in 'calling a spade a spade' and right away told us that she "wasn't in favour of missions." Mary was often embarrassed by some of the things she said. She wore a coarse hessian pinafore and clogs and you could hear her clattering across the yard and rattling her bucket as she went to feed the pigs or the calves.

On the first morning we were given a big farmhouse breakfast, then had a Bible reading and a prayer.

However, Martha walked out saying, "You get on with your praying while I get on with the work".

76

How the pastor's prayers were answered

At ten we met Pastor Snow at the chapel. He gave us a list of people for whom he had a particular concern and as we got to know these people ourselves we were able to pray specifically for individuals and their needs. Mary had asked us to remember Martha in our prayers and a number of people mentioned a club that met in an upper room in the local pub and particularly the leader, Harry. He had heard of us and he made it very clear that he wasn't interested and wouldn't be coming to any of our meetings.

On the Thursday morning Mary spoke to us about her sister, telling us of some of the hard knocks that she had received in life, which had made her bitter, preventing her from finding a faith that was real and a peace for which she longed. I knew that it would need a miracle to get her to come after all the things that she had said. So, when the two sisters walked in together, we were very surprised. I began the service and Bill preached. He gave a powerful word, several people came forward and, as we got to the last verse of the hymn we were singing, Martha - tears streaming down her face - came and knelt with the others. Later, before we went to bed, she joined Mary, Bill and myself as we prayed together. There was a different atmosphere in the home. She was a new woman and we felt that our mission had been worth it for Martha's sake - and Mary's. Martha told us openly that all her banter and scepticism had been a cover for her real need which she was too embarrassed to reveal.

Harry becomes a new man

On the last night Bill started the service and I went to see if there were any latecomers. Standing in the yard outside was Harry, looking very miserable and smoking a cigarette. I persuaded him to come in, which he did reluctantly, and sat at the back looking very much ill at ease. I preached that night and made an appeal. A number of people came forward with their different needs and last of all, Harry. It was costly for Martha to come, it was far more costly for Harry. Afterwards he invited us to his home to talk to him and his wife Mary and we had a lovely time with them. He became a keen member of the church and later studied to become a Local Preacher.

The Glory Chariot

I don't pretend to understand the mystery of prayer, but I'm absolutely convinced that it makes a difference and we saw evidence of this during the few days that we spent at Long Preston. People in the church were blessed but none more so than Bill Stubbs and me and this was a direct result of working with a man of prayer. Kenneth Snow was a humble man who had a simple but deep faith and before we left we came to realise that here was a spiritual giant.

He had very few of this world's goods, neither did he seek them, but he was the very proud possessor of a little Austin which he called 'The Glory Chariot'. Here is his story as he told it to us, "Some weeks before the mission I wasn't at all well and found it increasingly difficult to get round my churches on my bicycle, travelling miles in all sorts of weather. So I told the Lord, 'You'll have to help me or I can't continue'. The Lord said to me, 'You must have a car'. He knew and I knew that I had no money to buy one, but if the Lord tells you then you know that He will provide. In the village there was one garage, so off I went, and there on the forecourt was my car. It was a little Austin Seven with a price card on it for £120. So I saw the owner of the garage, who knew me, and told him that I would like the little Austin, and would he keep it for me until I had the money. He agreed and put SOLD on the car.

That afternoon I visited two ladies in the village who, in the course of the conversation, said to me, "Pastor, we're worried about you. You aren't looking well, and we feel it's far too much for you to go cycling all round the circuit; you need a car, and we would like to give you some money towards buying one". They then handed me an envelope, and *IT SO HAPPENED* (my capitals!) that it contained £l20. I couldn't thank them enough, and hurried home to tell my wife. Instead of rejoicing, she said, 'Kenneth, it costs a lot of money to run a car, and we just can't afford it'. I explained that the Lord knew exactly what money we needed to run the car and wouldn't provide one without the means to run it. So I went with the £120 to the garage. The owner came to greet me with a smile and said, 'Pastor, after you went from here the other day asking me to keep the little Austin for you, I had a 'phone call from two ladies telling me to tax and insure the car, and to put all the running expenses on their account".

So Pastor Snow got his car and Bill and I got a lesson in 'God Confidence' that we never forgot. By the way, Bill and I rode with him in the 'Glory Chariot', and we decided that it was safer for us to walk as we didn't feel that either of us was yet ready for 'Glory'! We both felt that it was a pity the Lord hadn't 'gone the extra mile' and provided him with a refresher course in driving!

CHAPTER SEVEN

THE GREAT TREK

The sermons most needed today are the sermons in shoes.
C. H. Spureon.

One of the vital parts of the training that Cliff College gave in 1946 was the Summer trek. Although I had to leave the trek early I still feel that it was most helpful. I learnt such a lot in such a short time, much more than I would have learnt by simply studying books. It was a good training in:

> relationships,
> discipline,
> faith,
> resourcefulness,
> humility.

It was Samuel Chadwick who first of all had this vision of sending men out as Christ sent his disciples out. When I first read about this, the idea appealed to me, but I never dreamed that one day I would become a Cliff College Trekker myself.

A Trek Leader

We had all just finished breakfast one morning when the Principal stood up and announced, "Will the following men see me in my study immediately". He then read out seven names, and mine was the first. We followed him into his study not knowing what to expect. He said

"I have called you men here because I want you each to lead a Trek team. It will not be easy, and so much will depend on you. We send you out as Jesus sent his disciples out, without food (except for the first day), without money and with the understanding that you do not ask for anything but a cup of water. You will go out in faith. You will take just those things that are necessary and nothing more, and you will sleep on the floors of such chapels where you find a welcome. It will not be easy for people to feed you for - as you know - food is rationed.

However, we believe that God will supply all your needs but not all your wants. The staff are sorting the men into teams later today, but I would like each of you to nominate the man you want to be Assistant Team Leader with you."

I chose Bill Stubbs.

Our Trek Team

Bill Stubbs. Bill and I had committed our lives to Christ in the same mission at Kelsall under the preaching of brother Tom Butler. Bill was a tower of strength to the team.

Fred Grange from Kings Lynn, Norfolk. During the war he had served on the King George V battleship. He did well with the children.

Harry Pickstock from Longton, Stoke on Trent was the oldest member of the team. We've kept in touch with each other regularly since then and he has preached for me many times.

Frank Hamlin from Gloucester was the youngest member of the team. A lovely lad. He kept our Trek Log.

We had three men in the team from Northern Ireland:

Frank Bolster from Dundonald, a faithful worker.

Bert Kelso from Dungannon. He was portly, a lover of Wesley's hymns and, at times, a day dreamer, but a lovely fellow.

Bob McCrea from Lisburn, had curly hair and was full of fun. The girls fell in love with Bob!

Days of preparation

I invited the whole team to come to my room that night, and told them that our team was number one, and our itinerary included Morecambe, Long Preston and back to Cliff by the end of August. I also said that we had the job of working out

Eric with a "latterday" trek cart

the route, (which I estimated would be 250 miles) and contacting those people on the route who might be able to help us by finding us a place to sleep. We had also to plan how to pack the clothes and cooking things that we would need, together with hymn books and a piano accordion, into our purpose built trek cart. In addition, we had to obtain a bicycle.

June 25th was the day when all seven teams set off. As that day approached we got more and more excited, and in some cases more anxious. I was under great pressure, because not only was I having to take a lead in planning, but on Monday July 1st I would have to leave the team to take my oral exam for the ministry. This was crucial for, although I had managed to get through my previous exams, I had only just scraped through. However I still held on to the belief that if the Lord meant me to be a minister and I did my part, then I would get through, and if I didn't, then He had something else in mind for me. I didn't worry, but I did work.

A leap into the dark.

One of the things that I remember Cliff for was the bells. There were bells five minutes before every meal, every service, every lecture and then a final bell on time. When the final bell rang we had to be in our place and woe betide the man who was late. This was good discipline training for the ministry. My room was on the top floor of the college and the time for evening prayers was approaching. I was busy trying on an extra pair of stockings in my trek boots when the five minute bell rang. I was late, and quickly changed into my socks and shoes and ran down the first flight of stairs, jumped down the second flight but as I landed I fell and twisted my ankle. I felt sure I had broken it. I managed to push my way back up stairs, hopped to my room and lay on my bed. That was a very dark moment for me. I was sick with pain and anxiety. This surely would prevent my going on Trek. I cried aloud, "Lord! Lord! Why?" It was, of course, my own silly fault. I had my ankle X-rayed; it wasn't broken but badly strained. I went round the College on crutches, and when the team set off I stood and waved them off, under the able leadership of Bill Stubbs.

Father, mother and Vera had come to watch the teams set off - North, South, East and West - and then took me home. I was feeling very sad, but encouraged when the doctor told me that with rest I might be able to walk in about a week.

The Trek Diary.

I am so very glad that I kept a diary of our Trek and it has been most helpful to me now as I have tried to recall those days. I have wished again and again that if only I had kept one all through my ministry, then my book would have been much fuller and more interesting. But then I never dreamt that I would be writing a book.

Bill and the rest of the team arrived at Warrington on June 28. As this was only about sixteen miles from my home I joined the team for two days. The Rev. Percy Robinson, who was the minister at Kelsall when Tom Butler missioned there, gave us a royal welcome.

The July Committee

July 1. I left the team to go to Hartley Victoria College, Manchester, for my July Committee Oral exam. There were twenty-five candidates (all men - no women in those days). In the evening we were each examined by a doctor, then attended evening prayers. The next day I had to wait around until 2.30 pm before I was called in to face the committee of examiners. Mine were Rev. Russell Shearer, Rev. Dr. Brewis (Principal of Hartley Victoria College) and the Rev. Wilfred Doidge; a well known leader in the church.

The exam lasted twenty minutes and then I went back home to the New Pale, where the family were anxious to know how I had got on. The next morning a self addressed letter arrived. Vera brought it for me to open. In it was a brief note saying, "THE COMMITTEE HAS RECOMMENDED THAT THE METHODIST CONFERENCE ACCEPT YOU FOR TRAINING FOR THE MINISTRY". When Vera read it, she flung her arms around my neck and gave me a kiss. I marvelled at the way the Lord had helped me every step of the way.

Back with the team again

July 3. I was now ready to join the team again, although still limping, but feeling that a very big burden had been lifted off my shoulders now that all my exams were over, and the many hurdles had been overcome.

July 4. Left Warrington at 8. 30 a m then on to Wigan along the busy road (no M6 then). My ankle began to pain me so I was given the bike.

On arrival at the Queens Hall we were all very tired. The ladies had prepared a meal for us and said that a large number of women had already gathered in the main Hall and were expecting us to speak to them at 2. 30 pm. It was then 2.15!

I asked the Deaconess who was in charge to open the meeting and said that we would come at 2.45. I then insisted that all the members of the team lie flat on the floor, with their feet lifted up a bit and remain completely relaxed. When we joined the ladies we sang the hymn

"Now thank we all our God,
With hearts and hands and voices;
Who wondrous things hath done,
In whom his world rejoices;
Who from our mother' s arms,
Hath blessed us on our way,
With countless gifts of love,
And still is ours today. "

I then asked each member of the team to tell us briefly just what influence their mothers had had on their lives. That meeting, which had not been planned, proved to be one of the most memorable of the whole Trek and some of the women said they would never forget it.

The men didn't find it easy to get up in the morning. Pulling a heavy trek cart for miles was hard work. In spite of this we managed to be on the road by 8.10 am. I was of course on the bike, and felt guilty about it, for the main purpose of the bike was to give different members of the team a 'rest' as we travelled. I went ahead and took with me facilities for brewing up and got the kettle boiling for when they arrived.

A memorable time in Preston

We arrived at Carey Street Baptist Church in Preston at 1.00 pm. The minister there was the Rev. Fred Wilson, who himself had been a Cliff Trekker before the war. One of his members had very generously arranged for us all to go to a cafe for a meal. This was much appreciated.

We were looked after well in Preston and on Sunday, Fred Grange and I were invited after the Sunday morning service to have lunch and tea in the home of the Assistant Chief Constable of Lancashire with his wife and two daughters. After lunch he insisted that I rested my foot. He bandaged my ankle firmly and said that he would get someone to see me next day about having an elastic stocking.

A memorable open air meeting

Over two hundred people attended the service at Carey Street Baptist on the Sunday night. Afterwards we had an open-air service. Crowds came. Several of us spoke, and gave a simple testimony and when Fred Wilson asked if there was anyone there ready to accept Christ as Lord of their lives, seven young people came forward. It needed a lot of courage for anyone to do that for there were those in the crowd who had been hostile and heckled us.

Included in that seven were two brothers. I went across to them and took them aside. The elder one was very moved and wanted to talk. I took them both to the church, and there in the vestry counselled the elder one first and helped him to make a firm commitment. His name was Gordon Sutcliffe and he came from Penwortham. He was studying to go into the Merchant Navy and expecting to go in the next few weeks. He was a fine young fellow of nineteen. I then spoke to his brother, Lawrence, who was sixteen. Both lads came from a good home and seemed most sincere.

Fruits of mission

I am leaving my diary for a moment, for I am now able to give you news of what happened to Gordon Sutcliffe. He with his brother came to see us off the next morning at 8. 15. and followed us on their bicycles for a few miles. Another Trek team came that way a fortnight later and Gordon followed them. Unfortunately he was knocked off his bicycle, and seriously injured. This accident put an end to his career in the navy. However, he went to Cliff College and eventually was accepted into the Methodist ministry. He had a very fruitful ministry, but sadly he died whilst still active in the work. Recently I visited one of the churches where Gordon ministered at Poulton le Fylde near Blackpool. I found that the Pulpit Bible had been given in his memory and the people still remember his ministry with deep gratitude.

Preston to Dolphinholme

July 8. From Preston We went to Dolphinholme to a lovely chapel where we received a warm welcome.

Dolphinholme was such a contrast to Preston, Wigan and Warrington - it was so very quiet and many of the people were farmers. The weather was very hot and we had come in the middle of the hay harvest. One or two farmers said that they would have come to our services but they were busy in the harvest. I suggested to the team that instead of visiting the isolated houses we should offer to help one or two of the farmers. They all thought this was a good idea, so I set off on the bicycle to find out where our help could be best used.

Riding a bike without hands.

I am embarrassed to write this next piece . . .

As I was riding along happily whistling one of our choruses, I put my hands in my pockets and rode 'no hands!' I'd done it many times when I was younger.

However, on this day it was a good road, I was going fast down hill and didn't notice a brick in the road. The front wheel hit the brick and the handle-bars turned at right angles. I went flying through the air and landed on the road. I lay for a while feeling battered and bruised. I was hurt, especially my pride.

Whatever would I say to the team?

I felt angry with myself and embarrassed. After a while I went back to the chapel and, although badly shaken, I had broken no bones and was able to carry on after a lie down. I confess here that I didn't tell the team the whole truth about how the accident happened. I simply said that I was riding happily along - which was true- when my front wheel hit a big brick in the road that I hadn't seen - which was also true - but I didn't add that I had my hands in my pockets at the time - 'Some mothers do 'ave 'em'.

The whole team, except me, went hay making and enjoyed it and their witness in the fields was good. All the village knew what they had been doing, and the folk at the chapel were very impressed. This was a 'language' that they could understand.

Don't leave a place as you find it!

Most of us will have been to a place where there was a notice "PLEASE LEAVE THIS PLACE AS YOU FIND IT". Now being a good Scoutmaster I always used to say to the lads "A good Scout always leaves a place better than he found it". That is what I told our team on Trek. "No matter how well we preach and how wonderful our testimony, if we leave a place dirty and don't show our gratitude to the folk, they will remember that more than our preaching". So - before leaving for Knott End - we made the place 'spick and span' by 8.00 am.

Knott End: an adventure with boys

We had a good journey, and wondered just what lay ahead.

This was to be a new adventure for all of us, and something quite different from the rest of the Trek. While we were in Warrington we had visited the Warrington Cottage Homes. The College had had a request from the matron asking if some of the students could help organise a camp for the children at Knott End near Fleetwood. Our team and the one following us were told to try and help. This was a home for boys and girls between the ages of seven and twelve. They came from a variety of homes but all the homes had one thing in common - trouble. Some of the children had been abused by their parents. Some had abused their parents when they got out of control. Some were being cared for while their parents, one or both, were serving prison sentences. Many had been in trouble with the police, but all of them needing to know that Jesus loved them.

The matron was Miss Platt, a very capable Christian lady and very strict. We came to admire her and marvelled at the way she managed to keep order. She told us that the tents would be up before we got there and that she wanted us simply to look after the boys; to entertain them, AND KEEP THEM OUT OF TROUBLE. Tents and food would be provided for us. We planned to have a form of morning prayers, with a good story, and then to divide them into four teams, with two of us working with each team and at the end of the day have a sing song, and some Bible stories. We thought it would be such a welcome change not to have to walk miles pulling the cart, then conducting Gospel meetings. This was going to be a nice holiday for us near the sea?

Camping capers

When we arrived at Knott End we soon found the camp. We approached it singing one of our marching songs,

> *"Onward Christian soldiers,*
> *Marching as to war,*
> *With the cross of Jesus*
> *Going on before."*

Matron got the children lined up ready to meet us, and we were thrilled to see a ready made audience.

After giving us a welcome, she explained that we would be looking after the boys most of the time - and she left, with the girls. One of the lads asked us if we were cowboys. They were anxious to see what we had in the trek cart and lifted the lid, and started to take things out. We very soon realised that our original plan of action wasn't going to work, so we decided to take them into the largest tent and get them to sit down. I then told them who we were and that we had come hoping to give them the best holiday of their lives, that we had lots of things for them to do and some special treats which included taking them to Blackpool Tower Circus. But they had to help us to help them, for Matron had warned me that if there was trouble, then these special treats would be cancelled.

Our own circus

It soon became clear to us that we didn't need to go to Blackpool to see a circus. These fifty two lads provided us with our own. They were up to all sort of tricks. I could write pages on some of the things that happened to us. But, at the end, the team all agreed that the lads had taught us far more than we ever taught them and we were all truly thankful for the week we had with them, even though at times we were at our wits end.

For example : Bob and Harry were passing an apple orchard with twelve lads. A kind gentleman asked if "the little boys would like to come in and pick a few of the apples that had fallen?". They not only picked a few that had fallen, but made sure that a whole lot more fell as they shook the branches and climbed the trees!

One of the lads with Frankie Hamlin threw a stone, just missed an old lady's head and smashed a bus shelter window. When crossing on the ferry one of the lads was missing. He had climbed up the side of the ship's funnel.

When some of them went into a chemist's shop to spend their pennies they came out with Solidex peppermint tooth paste and bars of Chocolax (a chocolate laxative). We need to remember that sweets were rationed. They ate the tooth paste as peppermint cream . . . and the Chocolax as chocolate!

Sidney

There was one lad who stands out in my mind. His name was Sidney. He was one of the older lads (eleven) and his nine year old brother was there too. Matron had spoken to me about Sidney. He had caused them more trouble than any other. She said he was very clever, very artful and needed to be watched at all times. I decided to take a personal interest in him and made sure that he was in my group. The lads were each given a little pocket money, but not Sidney. Matron gave his pocket money to me and said that he was not to have it if he had previously been in trouble.

One afternoon, while Fred Grange and I were out walking with our group of twelve, we came to an ice cream van. A queue had formed and they all wanted to join it, including Sidney. So far that day he had been good. He reminded me of this and I gave him two pennies for a cornet. I watched Sidney for Matron had said ". . . he has a habit of going into pockets that are not his own". He kept looking at me as he moved along 'as though butter wouldn't melt in his mouth'. When it was his turn, he handed over his two pennies and picked up the cornet. As he did so I thought I saw him knock something off the van ledge but I wasn't sure. He came to me happily sucking his ice cream and looking pleased with himself.

Sidney (standing) at camp with some of the boys.

"Sidney" I said, "did you pick something up off the shelf of that van?". He denied it. I felt his pockets - they were empty, but he was holding his ice cream up to his mouth, and his right arm close to his chest. I pulled his arm and the metal wafer- making gadget dropped on the floor.I returned it to the girl in the van and then asked Fred if he would take the rest of the group off on his own for I was going to take Sidney straight back to the camp and to Matron. The idea of being taken to Matron really upset Sidney. He kept pleading with me not to, so when we came to a quiet spot I decided that we would sit down and have a talk together. I was really puzzled why he should risk so much to take something that was of no use to him at all.

My Uncle Charlie never gets caught!

As we sat I asked him a number of questions, the first being who was his best friend. Without hesitation he said "My uncle Charlie". I then asked "What does your uncle do?".

"He's a burglar, like my dad, but Uncle Charlie never gets caught. He's very clever, and he used to teach me, before they took us away, after our mam was taken into clink for hitting me and our kid". He told me all this in such a matter of fact way, just as I might have said that my father was a farmer. I tried not to sound shocked or surprised. I then asked him just why he had taken the ice cream wafer maker. At once he replied, "Uncle Charlie told me, that if you are going to be good at your job, you need to keep practising and I just thought I ought to practise".

This was a quite new experience for me. I remembered it later when at Handsworth I was writing an essay on 'Christian Ethics' and trying to answer the question "How do you determine what is right and what is wrong?". To Sidney, taking that gadget wasn't stealing, it was doing what his favourite uncle wanted him to do - practise so that he could be good at his job later.

I must have spent more than one hour, sitting and talking to Sidney, and the more we talked, the closer I was drawn to him. He went on to tell me that his dad was "doing a long stretch", for attacking a policeman while on a job, something that his Uncle Charlie said "You should never do". He also told me that when his dad was taken away, his mother found it hard to feed all the family of four children - he was the eldest - and that when he came home from school she would often say to him. "Sidney, I've got no food and no money, there is nothing for tea for any of us unless you go and get it". And so this little lad would have to go out on to the streets of Liverpool on an "errand of mercy".

Was that right or was it wrong?

By this time Fred and the rest of our gang had come back, so we joined them and went into the camp together. Sidney again pleaded with me not to tell Matron. I had no intention of telling her for I couldn't honestly say that he had been a naughty lad.

Sidney demonstrates his skills.

I did however speak to her about him and some of the things that he had told me. She didn't know anything about Uncle Charlie, but she did know about his parents and said that what he told me was all true. She then went on to tell me about a hair-raising experience that they once had at the home in Warrington; how one day the police had arrived, reporting that a boy had been seen on the top of the tall building. He hadn't been missed, but when they went out they were horrified to see young Sidney actually standing on the very top. He waved his hand to them and demonstrated how he could walk across the apex of the roof. The police officer decided to call the fire brigade who eventually got him safely down, but not till Sidney had demonstrated some of his cat like skills. I think that his Uncle Charlie would have been proud of him that day!

At the end of each day our team got together and we shared with one another some of the things that had happened during the day. I told them about Sidney and all that he'd said. They were all very moved and we decided to pray especially for him. It certainly taught us all a vital lesson on the way we judge people and are quick to condemn without knowing all the motivating forces that had caused them to do the things that they did.

A Scout on duty

I was very glad that before going to Cliff College I had been a Scout Master as my training came in very useful at Knott End. One day I was able to make some 'savoury twists', over an open fire. The twists consisted of a mixture of flour, powdered egg and little bits of bacon or sausage all mixed together. The mixture was then cut into narrow strips about the length of a small sausage. These were wrapped round pieces of sturdy twigs which had been prepared for the job. Each child was given one which they had to bake over the fire. They loved these, but it was a slow job. I also gave them all a demonstration on how to make a cosy sleeping bag out of a single blanket by folding it a certain way. It was cold at night, and when we went round we often found some of them awake.

A kiss in the dark

The biggest problem that we faced on the camp - apart from how to keep the boys out of mischief, was caring for the old army tents when it was windy. They were much more difficult than our modern tents to deal with. Before going to bed when it was very bad, we all went round each tent, adjusting the ropes to the right tension, making sure that all the flaps were secure and that each tent was well pegged down all round. On this particular night a storm arose and I took my torch at about 2.30 am and went to check that everything was all right. One of the tent flaps had been opened and when I shone my torch inside I could see a little lad, his name was Simon. He was sitting on his bed sobbing, and he told me that he was frightened and cold. We'd been told that Simon had been abandoned as a baby. No one knew who his parents were or where he came from. I managed to make his blanket into a cosy sleeping bag and got him to get into it and snuggled down. I placed my hand on his head, said a short silent prayer and I was about to leave when he said "Hey, mister, haven't you forgotten something?". I didn't know what he meant. He lifted his face up towards me, and said "you never gave me a kiss". A great lump came into my throat as I bent over him, gave him a quick kiss and tucked him in his little bed. Simon had never known a father's care or a mother's kiss.

As the week went on, it was good to see the response from the lads. We were beginning to 'bond' with them. They began to trust us; we began to understand them and they looked forward to the 'Jesus stories' at night. I could see a real change in Sidney. He was much quieter and more anxious to 'be a good lad'. Every time we went out he would say as we got back "Brother Eric, will you tell matron that I've been a good lad?".

A sad farewell

The morning that we left was a memorable one. We were up at 6 am, got our trek cart loaded and our tents all cleared ready for the team who were coming later to take over from us. We were ready to leave at 8.00 am, before the children were up, but as it was a fine morning Matron allowed them all to come out in their pyjamas and to wave goodbye. I had a quick word, thanking Matron and the staff for their kindness, and telling the young people how much we had enjoyed being with them and that we would miss them.

From fear to faith

What a contrast to the day when we arrived. We were strangers then, keeping one eye on the lads and the other on all our property. Now there was an entirely different scene. Boys and girls were in little groups, some sobbing and calling to different members of the team to write to them. They were all sorry to see us go. The one thing that we'd been able to do over the week was to show them real love, especially in the last two or three evenings when there had been a wonderful atmosphere in the tents as different members of the team had emphasised the fact that they were all very special in God's sight. That Jesus did love them and that we loved them.

This is what was lacking in their lives - they were hungry for love. In those days we were able occasionally to give them a cuddle. They began to realise that we did love them and they tried hard to please us. There is a fundamental truth here.

A lesson we never forgot.

I think that my most treasured memory of that week was when young Sidney came running to me, sobbing, and in the midst of his tears said "Brother Eric, I'll be a good lad for Jesus". Sidney was one of the older boys who had signed a Decision Card indicating that he had "Decided to follow Jesus", and I had said that one of the things that means is that "You are promising to be a good lad for

Jesus". I promised to write to him and to send him a small New Testament for himself. This I did. I've often wondered just what happened to young Sidney Titcombe.

Thinking back to that week now after some fifty years, if ever a person deserved a medal, it was Miss Platt, the matron. She had a difficult job and she did it well. I believe that precious seeds were sown in the lives of some of those young people and our team learned lessons that we never forgot.

On the road again

We were all sad to leave the young people at Knott End and wished that we could have stayed another week, but the team that followed us had a great time and said that the youngsters were eager to listen from the very first day and they didn't have the behaviour problems that we encountered at first. It was good to hear this. However, we were happy as a team to be on the road again and heading for Morecambe. I was so thankful that my ankle had improved such a lot and that I was now able to march with the others.

The church at Morecambe where we were going to stay was Green Street and when we arrived we were very wet, having come through pouring rain on the last few miles. We were also very tired and thirsty. I decided that we'd all have an evening off, each doing his own thing. There were letters to write, and 'smalls' to wash *etc*. Our role at Morecambe was very much a supporting one. The 'Big Guns', all of whom were associated with Cliff College, came over to speak at the meetings and we took a secondary but important role. The speakers included Rev. George Allen, my most helpful tutor; Brother Tom Butler, Herbert

Eric preaching at Morecambe

91

The trekkers on the road

Silverwood, Fred Wilson from - Preston, Jack Bedford - minister from Carnforth, Rufus Booth with his piano accordion, Wallace Mason and Jim Etherington.

In addition there was a farmer friend, George Redrope, who travelled regularly from Farndon near Chester. He gave a lot of practical, and generous help to us. We held meetings morning, afternoon and evening. The evening Rally was special and we had as many as four hundred people there, the team was kept busy, counselling and following up enquiries.

Cupboards have ears

I have lots of memories from Morecambe, but one that stands out was something that happened to me the second Sunday afternoon that we were there. There was no meeting so we all had a free afternoon. The one thing that I wanted to do was to find somewhere where I could have a good sleep.

The trouble at Green Street was that we had no privacy. People were coming and going all the time. In one of the rooms where some of us slept, there was a huge cupboard with wide and deep shelves. I cleared one of these shelves, climbed in and pulled the door shut. It was ideal - at least so I thought - and I settled down for a good sleep. I was awakened when several girls in their late teens came looking for us. Our personal things were in this room, including photographs of family and girl friends. It was obvious that one of them had picked up a photograph of a girl and they were discussing whose girl friend it would be. They then started talking about the members of the team, and saying which they fancied. One said "I like Bob", another said "I think he's a bit flighty". Another said she fancied Frankie, but then he was "too young to be taken from his mother". Then one said "I like Eric, I think he's smashing". To which another said "I think he is too bossy, you should hear how he orders the team about sometimes!". They went on and on gossiping about us. The trouble was that these girls were actually standing just by the cupboard. If I bent my knees I would force the door open and if I sneezed I would blow it open. Any movement that I made they would hear. Fortunately for me a member of the team came back. One of the girls said that they had come round to enquire if they could help us in distributing the hymn sheets later that night at the "open air". If only those girls knew all that I knew about them. When I later told the team what had happened, some of them were anxious to know what was said about them and who said it. I didn't tell.

92

Herbert Silverwood

The man who was most able to draw a crowd and hold their attention in the open air was Herbert Silverwood. He had a powerful voice and a fund of funny stories that made people laugh. He would always end on a serious note, but it often took a long time to get there. He wasn't the easiest of people to share a meeting with for he was so unpredictable. But he was able to reach people who were out of the reach of most of us.

This is digressing, but later in my ministry my friend and colleague was the Rev. Ernest Foster and I happened to mention Herbert Silverwood to him. This is what he said, "I've never been so embarrassed in my life as I was when sharing a meeting with Silverwood. It was just after the war and I joined in an Ecumenical Commando Campaign in London. There were about fifty ministers from different denominations who took part. I was in a team of six. There were three Anglican vicars, a Congregational minister, Herbert Silverwood and me. We were sharing in an open air meeting in a busy Market Square. It was our first meeting together as a team and we were all nervous except Silverwood and he was going to speak last.

The rest of us each gave a brief word, but only a handful of people stopped to listen and then walked on. However when it came to Silverwood's turn he asked all the ministers to stand in a circle. He then saw a fellow who was walking past wearing a black bowler hat. He went to him, and asked him if he could borrow his hat just for a moment. The fellow very reluctantly handed it over, then Herbert borrowed a white handkerchief, from another reluctant donor. All this time the clerical brethren were getting more and more embarrassed, but not Herbert. He placed the white handkerchief on the ground and the black bowler on the handkerchief. By this time a few more people had stopped, wondering what these parsons were doing and what was under the hat. In less than five minutes a crowd of fifty had gathered and it grew and grew - folk thought that there must have been an accident.

Then Herbert spoke. He explained who we all were, why we were there and gave them a really helpful message. He then returned the hat and the handkerchief. He showed us how to get a crowd, but not one of us had the courage to do it".

A Sky-Lark sings!

August 10. After two weeks at Morecambe we were back on the road again, calling at Carnforth and Milnthorpe, and then on to High Bentham.

I quote from my diary.

'August 13. Milnthorpe. Up in the morning at 6.15 am, and we were on the road at 8.15. It's a great thrill to set out with the team on the open road, when the fields are still wet with dew and the Westmorland mountains are covered with a slight mist. As the day proceeds, the sun gets warmer, the mist disappears and a sky-lark sings.'

We were expecting a hard journey to High Bentham for there was a steep hill to go up and down. I suggested that we would begin our quiet time when we had done five miles and reached the top of the first hill. Just as we reached the summit, a big car stopped in front of us and a farmer whom we had met at Carnforth stopped. He was on his way to High Bentham market and suggested that we tied the trek cart to the back of his car, then all except the cyclist should get in - the car, not the trek cart! It was a real squash. Two of the lads sat in the boot, with their legs dangling out, holding on to the front of the cart. It was a good job that no police car came along. We were not only breaking the law of the land, but the unwritten rules of trekking, that trekking meant walking (except for the one cyclist). However, I must say I very much appreciated that ride and felt justified in accepting it as a 'work of grace'. As we reached the outskirts of High Bentham, we all got out and resumed our march, singing as we went through the market area and stopped just to tell the people there who we were, why we'd come, then invited them all to come to the Methodist Church at 7.30, and to tell the children that there would be a Sunshine Corner for them at 5.30.

Excuse me, would you like a bath ?

Later that afternoon, as I was walking round the market place a lady came to me and said, "Excuse me, I hope you don't mind me asking, but would you by any chance like a bath?"

Now under ordinary circumstances, I would have been offended if a complete stranger asked me such a question, but I was so very thankful to accept and went with her to her lovely home. She told me how pleased she was that the Trekkers had come again and how they had come regularly before the war. She remembered that one of the things that the men most appreciated was a good hot bath.

Bert (The Brake) fails

It was a lovely day when we left High Bentham and the first part of the journey was perfect, but we had a mishap. There were no brakes on the trek cart and it was heavy, and when going down hill there were two anchor-men on the back ropes whose job was to hold us back. Now Bert Kelso, who was the heaviest member of the team, was one of the anchor-men. This was a good place to be most of the time, but if the hill was steep then it wasn't. Bert was often 'in another world from us', day dreaming. Now this morning we came to go down a hill that wasn't too steep and the front team, feeling fit, began to trot. We continued to go faster and faster. Bert had made a large loop on his rope, and put it round his waist, and leaned back, trying to act as a brake on the cart. But the rope slipped from his waist and down behind his knees. By this time we were going too fast and poor old Bert was dragged off his feet - but his weight dragging along the road did enable us to stop. It was a miracle that he wasn't badly hurt. Although shaken, he was able to continue after changing his shorts which had a huge hole in the seat.

This caused us to be more careful going down the hills, but I'm afraid we couldn't stop laughing at the spectacle of poor old Bert trying to hold us back, then being dragged along like a bag of flour. Looking back I don't think there was another period of my life when I did more laughing than we did on that trek. The Irish are noted for their humour and the three lads on our team certainly caused us much laughter, especially Bert and Bob McCrea.

Real Yorkshire pudding.

It was twenty miles from High Bentham to Long Preston, and we were by this time beginning to feel hungry and planning a lunch stop, when Jim Towler, a young farmer from Long Preston came in his car to meet us. He told us that in less than half a mile, if we called at a farm, we would be provided with a lunch. This was wonderful news and we again began to trot. When we arrived we had a warm welcome from Mr and Mrs Fawcett, who had been supporters of Cliff for years, and when they knew that we would be passing they prepared for us a good hot dinner of roast beef and Yorkshire pudding. It was the best meal that we had on the whole of the Trek. We were so very hungry. Mrs Fawcett gave each of us a big plate of Yorkshire pudding and gravy. I've never tasted better, and thinking that this was the main meal, when she asked if we would like some more, several of us said "yes please".

While we were eating our second helpings to our amazement she brought in a huge piece of roast beef, potatoes, carrots, and gravy, and told us to keep our plates. Mr Fawcett carved the beef and our plates were filled. We struggled through that, then afterwards she came back with apple pie and custard. When we told some friends about this later they laughed and said that it was an old Yorkshire custom to serve Yorkshire pudding as a separate course. Originally the idea was to satisfy hungry men folk, so that they wouldn't want so much expensive meat. We certainly enjoyed it, but we were a bit sluggish afterwards and it took us a mile or two before we really got going.

I couldn't help thinking of when Principal Broadbelt had explained that we would go out in faith, as the disciples went out "asking for nothing but for a cup of water", and the fears that some of our parents and friends had. "Remember" they said, "food is not as plentiful as it was before the war". Apart from that very first week, before I joined them, we never wanted for anything. God supplied all our needs, and we were able to send a generous donation back to the college.

Welcome back to Long Preston.

We went on to Settle where a group of young people had come by bus from Long Preston to meet us with the idea of marching with us back to Long Preston. When we were about a mile off we decided to start jogging. At first the young folk kept up with us, but then we kept going faster and faster and before long we left them behind.

We arrived at the chapel, a place of happy memories for Bill Stubbs and me, and were met by Pastor Snow and *surprise,* also the Principal of Cliff, the Rev. J. A. Broadbelt, and Brother Tom Butler. They were glad to see us all looking so fit after such a journey and that we were able to run as we did that last mile. The young people arrived later and they were most impressed that we had been able to run so well at the end of a twenty mile journey. I was surprised too and it illustrated for me the secret of how athletes get so fit - they train.

To be back in Long Preston was a real thrill for Bill and me. It was good to meet 'Mary and Martha' and Harry Humphries and his wife Mary again, and to know that he was training to be a Local Preacher. It was at this point that I had to leave the team to go home and get ready for my first appointment as a minister. After the final service, Mr Robinson, a farmer from Bells Farm, Caton, took me to his home and the next day he took me all the way home to the New Pale.

From Long Preston, Bill, who led the team at the beginning because of my bad ankle, now took over again and led them all the way back to Cliff, through Ilkley, Bradford, Middlestown, Goldthorpe and Norton arriving at the College on Tuesday August 27th.

I was so thankful to God for the wonderful way he had supplied all our needs. *IT SO HAPPENED* again and again that the right people, were in the right place, just at the right time, and all these many happenings helped to build up our GOD CONFIDENCE. There is nothing more important than this.

CHAPTER EIGHT

FROM PIT BOTTOM TO MOUNTAIN TOP

A ministry that is college trained
But not Spirit filled
Works no miracles.

Samuel Chadwick.

"1946 and all that"

The year 1946 was a very memorable one for me. After a very remarkable series of *"It so happened"* events at the beginning the year I found myself a student at Cliff College, a Bible College with an emphasis on evangelism. Here I completed my candidate's studies for the Methodist ministry and from Cliff I took my final written exams and went to Chester for my oral exams. At the beginning of my second term at Cliff I was appointed the Vice-Chairman of the college and the leader of an eight-man trek team. While I was on trek, I received a message asking me to 'phone home. When I did Mavis, who helped mother in the house, answered and told me a telegram had arrived. She read it out but had difficulty in pronouncing the place name. This is what she read: "CHALLONER ERIC. REPORT TO ASHBY-DE-LA-ZOUCH. LETTER TO FOLLOW". I'd never heard of it and thought that it sounded like some place in French West Africa but a friend told me it was Ashby, in Leicestershire. I was to go for a year as a probationer before going into college.

The 'Letter to follow' came from the senior circuit steward in the Coalville and Ashby circuit, informing me that I would be lodging with Mr and Mrs Williamson, Sunnyside, Bosworth Road, Measham. Both father and mother were interested to see Measham and to meet Mr and Mrs Williamson, so they took me over for a preview and at the same time took some of my clothes and books. Mrs Williamson gave us a very warm welcome. I then went back to the New Pale for a week and finally left for Measham on my motor bike on 31st of August 1946.

"Does the minister live here?"

I arrived at Sunnyside at 4.30 pm and had just had a cup of tea and begun to sort out my things when the door bell rang. Mrs Williamson, who was in the kitchen, asked me to see who it was. It was a young woman who enquired "Does the minister live here?" I replied "I'm sorry, no!". From the kitchen Mrs Williamson called "He does" and came out laughing and explained that I'd only just arrived.

I felt embarrassed and when she said that she had come to see if she could have her baby christened on the following Sunday morning, I had to do some quick thinking. Although I had been to Cliff College this was not a training college for ministers and the course didn't include such practical matters as baptisms, weddings and funerals etc. I asked her a few questions, wrote a few details, said a prayer of thanksgiving for the little one and off she went.

"Don't drop the baby"

After she left, Mr Williamson, who was a miner and on the night-shift at the pit, got up from his bed and came downstairs. Mrs Williamson told him what had happened and they both had a good laugh. After our evening meal I went at once to Ashby to see the Rev. Edgar Crocker, who was the second minister in the circuit, the Superintendent minister being eight miles away at Coalville.

Mr Crocker was very helpful. The first thing he said was "Don't drop the baby! Hold him in such a way that he'll feel secure in your arms". He gave me some helpful literature and I went back much happier and more ready for my very first baptism. The service on the Sunday went well and everyone seemed to appreciate it except the baby, who yelled his little head off, in spite of the fact that I didn't drop him.

Minister on probation

Measham was just one of my eight churches, the others being Ibstock, Heather, Snarestone, Normanton, Oakthorpe, Moira and Shackerstone. In addition to having pastoral charge of all these churches, I had probationary studies to do and exams to take as well as all the services and meetings to prepare for. It's no wonder that in my diary for those days I often recorded 'Feeling very tired, finding it hard to cope', but I did, with God's help and a lot of hard work.

Living and working with miners

My home base was excellent and Mrs Williamson proved to be a 'mother in Israel'; so very caring and a good cook. Her husband, Dan, had worked down the pit all his life and was now a check weighman whose job was to see that the men had a 'square deal'. I became very fond of Dan. He was a man of integrity. I wish that I could remember all the many stories that he told me about his early experiences down the pit and how men had suffered at the hands of some of their bosses.

A canary comes to church

At my first service at Oakthorpe, which happened to be their Harvest Festival, there was on the table in front of the pulpit, in addition to fruit and vegetables, a lump of coal, a miner's lamp, a helmet, a pick axe and a canary in a cage. Canaries were taken by miners down the pit and were used to test for gas. At the first whiff of gas, the canary would fall off it's perch; that was a signal there was gas about. It would quickly revive with a breath of fresh air.

98

During the service I told them I had worked on the farm for ten years, but was completely ignorant about the business of mining and suggested that it would be helpful if I could have some experience of working down a pit. Afterwards, Albert Toon came to me and asked me if I was serious about wanting to go down the pit, and I said that I was. At that time, young men who were due to be conscripted into the army could elect to go into mining instead. They were called 'Bevan Boys' and *IT SO HAPPENED* that Albert Toon's job was to put these young men through a very brief period of training to see if they were suitable for the job. He offered to take me down the pit, to give me a taste of what it was like to be a miner

Going down the pit!

I was keen on the idea and so on a very cold November morning I met Albert at the pit top at Donisthorpe. I had put on overalls to cover my clothes and to keep me both clean and warm. He took me into the lamp house and fitted me up with my helmet to which he fixed a lamp and a battery to power it which was hung round my neck.

News had got round that the young parson was coming to see what it was like to work down a pit (I heard this afterwards) and the fellow in control of the winding gear knew, for as soon as we had stepped into the lift cage and shut the door Albert said "Mr Challoner, you'd better hold on; we're going to drop three hundred yards and we get to the bottom quite quickly". That was a gross understatement! We dropped like a stone and I felt I had left my stomach at the top. It took me a while to get over that drop.

The cost of coal

Albert then explained that we were going to walk to the coal face. He wanted me to experience just what it was like walking to work from the pit bottom. At first it was quite well lit, but as we made our way along the track it got darker and

darker, until the only light we had was that on our helmets which pierced the darkness straight ahead.

He gave me a stick to help me keep my balance when the track was uneven. We walked at the side of the rails and at intervals a truck loaded with coal would appear out of the darkness - no lights, no engine - but it was attached to a powerful moving steel cable which pulled it to the pit shaft bottom.

I kept very close to Albert, for I don't mind admitting I was frightened and felt safer close to him. However, what I hadn't expected was that the track would have a layer of fine dust covering it. This was to help prevent sparks from flying off the rails and causing an explosion if there was gas about. Every step that Albert took, he kicked up a cloud of dust and soon my eyes were smarting, my nose was blocked and I was thoroughly miserable. He'd said that it was about two miles to the coal face. It was the longest two miles I have ever walked and when we arrived at last, I was ready to drop.

In fact I did drop and sat watching the long row of men stripped to the waist, shovelling the coal on to the conveyer belt. The work was strenuous and they were sweating and their backs were covered with a black slime. After a rest I tried to speak to one or two men, but it was so very noisy. I couldn't recognise any of them but Albert introduced two of them, Bernard Christian and Doug Burbidge, both regular members of the Oakthorpe chapel. Following my visit to that pit face I just marvelled when these two young men came to a weeknight meeting, looking clean and fresh.

My visit to the pit face helped me to understand the people, not only the miners but their families too. It also helped me to be more sympathetic to those miners who went on strike, when it was decided to pay them only for what they did at the pit face and took no account of the effort of getting there. I never grumbled again about the price of coal.

A few weeks later I was preaching at Hugglescote and had lunch with a miner and his family. When I described my experience to him he laughed: "Donisthorpe is a 'Bevan Boy' pit. It's dry and has a coal face ceiling over four feet high. Where I work, it's a wet seam and has a ceiling sometimes only just thirty inches, which means that we have to crawl to the face and lie on our sides to shovel the coal and most of the time water comes dripping on to us".

Group of miners at the pit head

I just can't imagine working in such conditions. It wouldn't be allowed today. Whenever these miners came and knelt at the communion rail and held out hands, scarred by their hard and dangerous work, to receive the Bread and the Wine, I felt so very privileged to minister to such men.

The dreaded fall

When the coal is dug out each day, the night shift has to come and place pit props in position to hold the roof up. If this job isn't done quickly and efficiently then there's a fall and any men underneath are trapped. This is something that all miners and their families dread.

I hadn't been at Measham one month when news came through that there had been a fall in the Moira pit. The pit head sirens sounded. Rescue teams rushed in and anxious wives and families rushed to the pit-head for news. I went over at once, for many of the men from my church at Moira worked down that pit. These were the men who formed the famous Moira Male Voice choir. Lawrence Bourne, my senior steward at Moira, was one of them. When I got to the pit-head, only rescue workers and ambulance personnel were allowed beyond the barrier. However, when they saw my clerical collar I was allowed in.

The waiting was terrible. There were happy re-unions as men who were safe came up and then the first injured man came up on a stretcher and was put straight into an ambulance and taken to Burton Infirmary. Several came bandaged, but able to walk. Then another injured man came up on a stretcher. It was Lawrence Bourne who was rushed straight off in the ambulance. After seeing Mrs Bourne, I went to Burton Infirmary. Lawrence was in intensive care and critically ill.

It was announced on the wireless that there had been a fall at the Moira pit and that many miners had a miraculous escape. No-one had been killed, but three seriously injured and a number of others with minor injuries. Many men had been cut off for a time, but all had now been released. There was a great feeling of relief. It could have been so very much worse. However, Lawrence Bourne's serious injuries kept him several weeks in hospital. He was never fit enough to go down the pit again, but was able to resume his duties in the church and to take his place in the choir

Tom Butler

I very soon realised that there was a great opportunity for mission in the Measham, Moira and Oakthorpe churches, but knew that it wasn't possible for me to do it and at the same time continue my studies and all my other work. I wrote to Tom Butler and asked him if he would be willing to come over for a week-end mission at Moira. He was happy to do so and on Saturday 30th November 1946 he arrived at Sunnyside at the beginning of a very memorable weekend.

Tom Butler

The folk at Moira were most impressed, not only when he spoke in the pulpit, but visited them in their homes. On Saturday night he told us of some of his adventures during the war. He preached several times on Sunday and invited every one to come to the final rally on the Monday night. I had told him about Lawrence Bourne, who had been so seriously injured in the pit fall and he insisted on going to see him, on Monday morning.

Tyres from heaven

On the way to the hospital one of his tyres burst and his spare one was not safe. In order to appreciate the significance of what happened next, we need to remember that in 1946, tyres were very difficult to get. We went to three garages and were told the same story at each "to get a tyre you must get a tyre permit and to get a permit you must show that you are on vital work and that could take a few days". The situation seemed to me to be hopeless. But not to Tom. "Eric", he said, "we must pray about this" and he pulled to the side of the road. "We are on the Lord's business There is no work in the world more vital than this. He wants us to go to this hospital. He wants us to be at the Rally tonight and it's vital that I get back to Cliff tomorrow. Without a tyre we can't do these things. We can't get a tyre, but God can." I was anxious, but he was confident. We began to move on slowly towards the hospital. Ahead of us we could see some tall factory chimneys. *IT SO HAPPENED* that those chimneys belonged to the huge Pirelli tyre factory. Tom was over the moon. "We can't buy tyres at a tyre factory" I said. "They can only be bought through one of their agents".

"Eric" he said, "our *AGENT* will get them for us, come on!". Without hesitation, he drove up to the huge gates of this factory. They were closed. The security guard came to us, to ask what we wanted. Tom said "I'm wanting to speak to the Managing Director, he doesn't know that I am coming, but I am involved in some vital work, with my colleague, the Rev. Eric Challoner. A crisis has arisen and we need his help". The security guard didn't seem to be impressed. He simply said "Unless you have an appointment I can't let you through these gates". Tom then went on, "I'm very sorry to put you on the spot like this, but it is urgent, will you put me through to his secretary and I'll ask her advice". The man agreed to do this, but just before he 'phoned Tom asked him "By the way, what is her name?" I forget now just what it was but we will call her Miss Hickson.

The guard got through and told her, "There are two gentlemen here who wish to speak to you". He then handed the 'phone to Tom, who said "Is that Miss Hickson? Good morning. I am Mr Tom Butler of Cliff College and with me is my colleague, the Reverend Eric Challoner and I am involved with him in some vital work amongst the miners of Moira. We desperately need two tyres, in order to continue that work today and the one person who can help us is the manager himself". She had a word with him and then told Tom that the managing director had asked his deputy to deal with us. All this time the security guard was watching us with suspicion. Miss Hickson then asked to speak to the security guard and told him to let us through and direct us to the deputy chief, who listened as Tom explained why our mission was urgent. What happened next was a miracle. This fellow picked up his 'phone and asked a local agent to come and collect two tyres.

It's not what you know but who you know that matters

The agent came and we followed him to his garage (one of those we had already been to). He was truly amazed that we had managed to get tyres from the factory in this way. Brother Tom's parting words were "Friend, it's not what you know, but who you know that matters!". But on this occasion we didn't stop to explain *Who* it was that had helped us in this way.

A mission to miners

After Tom Butler's visit I wrote to Principal Broadbelt about the possibility of having a team of Cliff students to follow up the work started by his visit. He agreed and on February 9th Bill Stubbs, Ernest Steele and Arthur Harris arrived, all mature students, who later became Methodist ministers. The mission was heralded by heavy snow storms. I recorded in my diary on February 10th 1947 "Never for fifty years have conditions been so bad". In order to get to Moira Methodist Church on Sunday morning a team of miners were out early to cut a way through the snow. In places it was over eight feet deep. I walked from Measham to Moira, with Bill Stubbs. Fifty five adults and thirty three children came. For eight days the mission continued and the snow continued and the men went back to Cliff on Monday February 18th.

On the following Friday, without any warning (I didn't have a telephone in those days) I received the following telegram from the Principal of Cliff "EXPECT STUBBS, STEELE, HARRIS AND BEESLEY". Nothing more. All four arrived in the centre of Oakthorpe on the Saturday afternoon. I forget now just how they got there, but we were told that they had all been booked to conduct a mission somewhere else and that the folk there had cancelled it because they were snowed up so they were sent to us! What they didn't know, and as a matter of fact I didn't know either, was that the folk at Oakthorpe were having to cancel their services because they had run out of coke for the church boiler and the whole system was going to be drained. *IT SO HAPPENED* that late on Saturday night a huge load of coke was dumped outside the church. I never found out where it came from, or who paid for it. All that I know is that the services continued for over a week and great blessing resulted. There were those who said "never has our church been so blessed".

Within the church there had been deep family feuds. These were healed. In the church there were few people who would accept any office and so the same folk kept the same jobs year after year and there was no growth. After the mission we were able to launch out with a number of new meetings and what's more had a good team of people to run them. A weekly Youth fellowship was formed with a membership of sixty.

Another year

I had been sent to the circuit for one year, before going to Handsworth College, Birmingham, but stayed for two because they had no one at the end of my first year to replace me.

Following the missions at Moira and Oakthorpe and then yet another at Measham the work increased. I needed someone to share in this work with me. The person that I wanted and who was most suitable for the job was Bill Stubbs. Bill had shared in the missions and now he was spending another year at Cliff, on the evangelistic staff, and at the same time studying for the ministry. My idea was that he should come to us, study for his exams in the mornings and spend his afternoons and evenings sharing with me in the work. He was keen and *IT SO HAPPENED* he was available. The Principal released him and we provided him with lodgings and a wage. He did a fantastic job and was such a help to me personally. During the year he took all his exams and was accepted for the Methodist ministry.

Going back to college

Having had two hectic years in charge of eight churches and having been given the freedom to do my own thing, I found it a very big change, packing up and going into college. It was like going back to school. I'm glad now that I didn't go straight from home, for having had experience of the work, I now knew what to expect and what to train for. However at first I was very disappointed. So much of the time it seemed to me that the studies we were doing had no relevance at all for the sort of work that I had been involved in. For me personally, as a non-academic person, I found that the Greek and Hebrew was overwhelmingly difficult and unsatisfying, although some of my fellow students got a great deal from it and said that it was a great help to them in their spiritual life. This surprised me.

Jesus shows us how it should be done

When Jesus was here in the flesh, he took twelve men and spent two or three years with them teaching and preparing them for their ministry. They went where he went, they saw what he did. and as they went he taught them. Then he sent them out on mission and they had to come back and report just what had happened. He didn't isolate them from the people for any length of time, but went with them, amongst the people.

Instead of sending student ministers to a residential training college for three years, we could select from every District one or two gifted ministers who had been successful in their work and invite them each to take over the responsibility for training one, two or three students? Every few weeks - say six - the team, including their leader, would join other teams from Monday to Friday at one of our conference centres such as Willersley Castle, for prayer, fellowship and teaching.

What about our huge colleges? After prayerful consideration I would phase them out. Now I know this is but a dream and in reality there would be many administrative problems, especially because, these days, families are involved. But I think that it's worth considering. It would probably be much less expensive and it's based on the method that Jesus used.

The 'Rams'

What was it like in college? The first year students were called 'Rams' and second and third year students were called 'The Rest'. They didn't explain why we were Rams, but it might have something to do with the incident in the life of Abraham, when he showed himself willing to sacrifice his precious son Isaac, but God provided a ram instead. We were the rams ready to be sacrificed. That's just my surmise.

The mock test

In our first week all the 'Rams' were told to assemble in the main hall for a 'Test'. I can't remember the details, but we were supervised by one of 'The Rest'. When we finished we handed our papers in and that was the last we saw of them. No results were published.

The 'Rams' versus the 'Rest'

This race, we were told, was to, compare our fitness with the 'Rest'. It involved a cross country run, starting from the main hall, a distance of 'x' miles and returning to the hall. All the students were involved in this and we all assembled in running shorts and trainers. 'The Rest' were given five minutes start, and we were released one by one. There were arrows to guide us for the first mile.

We caught up with two stragglers and then we lost the signs and we Rams got lost in the 'far country'. Eventually we all found our way back to college, tired and dejected, only to find 'The Rest' changed and having afternoon tea in the hall.

These wretched folk (except the two stooges)had simply run through the front gate and then round to the back of the college.

The 'Rams' photograph

All the first year were asked to assemble on the steps in front of the main entrance. The 'photographer' asked us to shout as loud as we could, "CHEESE". At that moment several of 'The Rest' who had climbed up on to the balcony above us, emptied bags of flour down. We were then ordered 'to clean up our mess'. I must say I felt very bad about all this, indeed very angry, and just could not see the point of any of it.

However, when I became one of 'The Rest' and a new intake of 'Rams' arrived I was one who took part in these, 'ramifications'. Why? One of the things that most ministers need to guard against is becoming pompous and perhaps it did us good to be 'knocked off our perches'. I thought it might do others some good, so I took part, but I still have my doubts. .

The "Footballer of the Year"

At that time I was proud to count amongst my acquaintances Joe Mercer who was captain of Arsenal and also of England and had been chosen Footballer of the Year, by the Sports Writers Association. My sister Vera was bridesmaid at Joe's wedding and he and his wife Nora had visited us at the New Pale. When he knew that I was in college in Birmingham he said, "Eric, if you want to come to a match when we are playing in Birmingham, let me know and I will get you tickets". I only availed myself of this privilege twice, once when I took Sheila and once my friend Roy Dew. We were the envy of the whole college.

The college fire brigade

One of my outstanding memories is of the college fire brigade . . .

The college had fire fighting equipment, but no one had been placed in charge. Knowing that Howard Booth at one stage during the war had been a Fire Officer, I suggested to him that he ought to form a fire fighting team. He was happy to do this and organised a team of six of us. This met with the approval of the Resident Tutor.

Howard took his duties very seriously. He gave each member of his team a specific job to do and mine was to go to the main hydrant at the top of the stairs. This was housed in a glass fronted cupboard, with coils of fire hose and a jet. The main water supply came from this point and it was my job to turn it on.

He fitted each of us up with a tin hat on which the word FIRE had been painted in red. He also found a huge handbell and this, with the words FIRE BELL painted on it, was placed in a strategic position.

Fire fighting demonstration

On Saturday 3rd of December 1948 it was announced that the college fire brigade would be giving a demonstration immediately after lunch and all students and staff had to attend. I ought to say that in the long history of the college there had never been a fire.

Howard and his team, all in tin hats, were trying to look serious when the rest were laughing. Howard emphasised that this was a serious exercise and that no one must ring the fire bell unless there was a fire. He then introduced each member of his team explaining what we had to do. The fire bell was rung and we gave our demonstration.

That was at 1.45 pm on Saturday December 3rd.

The college fire

On Monday, December 5th at 11.30 pm, I was fast asleep and was awakened by someone ringing the fire bell and shouting as loud as he could FIRE! FIRE! FIRE! It was Ricky Jay. Howard's room was next door to mine. He came out and I can see him now, in his pyjamas and bare feet, standing in the corridor and shouting, "Who the devil is ringing that bell?"

Ricky came running, holding the fire bell and looking very frightened, and cried, "Honest, Howard, there IS a fire, it's in number 63, Roy Smith's den". As Howard ran towards No. 63 I grabbed a big fire extinguisher from its stand and followed him. He opened the door. It was like a blazing furnace. He shut it quickly and told the team to get to their places. I ran to my hydrant stand at the top of the stairs and got the main hose and jet out and Howard grabbed it, as he had done on the previous Saturday. He ran outside to the window of No. 63, broke the window with the jet and I turned on the water. The Birmingham Fire Brigade arrived thirteen minutes later. By this time, because the fire had been confined to the one room and Howard had been able to direct the full force of water into the confined space, most of the fire was out.

The Fire officer congratulated Howard and his very efficient team. He said the fire had been so fierce that, had it not been tackled promptly and efficiently, the whole college could have been threatened. The next day the headline of the Birmingham Post was "COLLEGE FIRE FIGHTERS CONGRATULATED" and there was a picture of the Resident Tutor and some of the team.

Looking back on this remarkable event - especially the timing of it, I think that we can include it as an *IT SO HAPPENED* event.

By the way; when I was at Cliff College we had often prayed, "Lord, Send the Fire" (the Fire of the Holy Spirit, that is). At Handsworth I continued to pray this prayer; but I didn't expect a fire like this one!

Handsworth College

This account so far of my time in College is very biased and isn't a true picture either of the College or of my time there. It's true that at first I wasn't very happy, but I soon settled down and found new friends, and was so glad to have the opportunity to study my Bible and to read; something that I'd not been able to do in the past.

Each student had his own den (study) with his bedroom above. Each den had an open firegrate, and we were allowed one bucket of coal each week. Incoming students were asked to form 'firms' - that is a group of four or five men who met together for fellowship and discussion and mid morning coffee breaks in each other's den. Occasionally we had a meal together. When I went home mother always sent me back with home cured bacon and a good piece of ham, which I shared with the firm. On such occasions we were the envy of the College for as we fried the succulent pieces of ham the aroma drifted along the corridors. Each

Handsworth College

firm had a name - we were 'The Farmers Boys' and we had a picture of 'Old farmer Giles' on our doors. The Principal was Dr. Howard, a man of authority and much learning. Each tutor had his own Class Meeting and I was in Dr Howard's. I found them most helpful. He was able to make the Bible live. He had a fantastic memory and was able to 'skip read' a thick book in an evening. As he turned the pages he was able take in a whole paragraph at a glance. If he wanted to refer to a book he could remember not only about what page it was on, but also what part of the page.

OLD GAFFER

FARMERS BOYS

I didn't take either Greek or Hebrew, which meant that I had more time to study other subjects. The highlights of my two years in College were Sheila's monthly visits. For these occasions in Winter I would save my coal and cook a good mixed grill. The time always went too quickly, and on several occasions she almost missed her last bus home.

Although I did eventually enjoy College life, I was longing to get back into circuit, and also to getting married.

CHAPTER NINE

THE BLESSINGS OF MARRIAGE

Marriage is more than finding the right person,
It is being the right person.

Anon.

On August 16th 1997 we celebrated for the 47th time our Wedding Anniversary. We had a lovely day together and I think that it is true to say that although we have had a very happy married life we have never been happier together than we are now and never more in love. That doesn't mean that we haven't had our problems - we have had many - but we have always come through them together. I read recently that two of the basic causes for marriages to break up are boredom and bills. I can't ever remember us being bored and we have adopted a life style that has enabled us to pay our bills.

Sheila asks me for a date
The very first time that Sheila spoke to me was as secretary of the Wesley Guild

Eric and Sheila celebrating their engagement at Rhyl. 1949.

at Measham, where I first began my ministry. She asked me if I was free the following Wednesday to preside at the annual meeting. I was free and I was most impressed with my Guild secretary. However I kept those thoughts strictly to myself. Mrs Williamson, my good landlady, was very fond of Sheila and her parents and would often say "Sheila Thirlby is a lovely girl", and she would try to find some excuse either for me to take a message from her to Sheila, or her mother. I didn't need an excuse but I did need to restrain myself from going too often and I confess that I was very concerned when I thought another fellow was also 'taking an interest in her'.

My pillion passenger

When her mother went into hospital in Burton, I visited her as her minister and asked Sheila if she would like a lift to the hospital as a pillion passenger. She readily accepted. I was nervous as I sat astride my bike, with Sheila, for the first time, behind me. I carefully put her feet on the pillion pedals and told her to get as close as she could and to lean forward on me. (This is the correct way for any passenger to sit). I still remember the thrill of that first ride that we had so close together. She was an ideal pillion passenger. At that time I had only a few weeks before going to Handsworth College, Birmingham. So after saying a fond farewell to my friends in the different churches where I had ministered for two years, I went home to the New Pale and got ready for College.

Popping the question

I was glad that Handsworth was the college chosen for me for it meant that Sheila could get a bus from her gate to Birmingham and catch a No 11 up to the college. She came about once a month and we both looked forward to those visits. It was during one of them that, after going for a walk, we went into the college chapel and knelt together in front of the cross and there I asked her if she would marry me. She simply said, "*YES*", and we then offered our lives to God, together. Then we went into the vestibule of the chapel and had a long loving kiss.

I knew that this decision would mean a big change for her parents. She was their only daughter and had never left home, except when she went to Goldsmiths College, London University, which was evacuated to Nottingham during the war. They were going to miss her very much, so I wrote and told them of my love for Sheila and that I had asked her to marry me, that she had agreed and I trusted that this would meet with their approval. They gave us their blessing and on Easter Sunday 1949 we formally announced our engagement.

The long wait

In those days ministers weren't allowed to marry while on probation and in college. Now many of them are married before coming to college and that includes women ministers, and they are provided with accommodation for their spouses and children! The earliest that we were allowed to get married was August 1950. This meant quite a long engagement, which in some ways was difficult for us. But we did what we believed God wanted us to do knowing that His way is best. I am sorry for young people today. They face peer pressures and media influences that we never had to face and many are being encouraged to follow a way of life that leads to frustration and boredom.

Counting the days

When the date of our wedding was fixed we made a pact that at 7.15 every morning, we would remember each other wherever we were and we would read from the (old) Methodist Hymn Book the hymn whose number corresponded with the number of days that we had to wait before our wedding day. So when there were still 52 days to go we read hymn number 52, "O love of God, how strong and true"; 12 days to go, No. 12, "Praise, my soul, the king of heaven"; and on our wedding morning No 1. "Oh for a thousand tongues to sing my great Redeemer' s praise".

Our Wedding Day

It was for both of us a wonderful day. We were full of hope and happy anticipation. The sun shone and it felt as though God was smiling on us. We were married in the church where Sheila had worshipped all her life; the church where I first began my ministry. The presiding minister was a personal friend of her father, Rev. J. J. Perry, assisted by the Ashby minister Rev. G. D. Clarke. Our best man was my close friend in college, Roy Dew. I had been best man for him and Olive just two weeks before. Sheila wore a white wedding dress and that had a true symbolic significance. I wore a black suit and that had no symbolic significance!

Our honeymoon

We went for our honeymoon to Porlock in Somerset and stayed in a small guest-house, They only had one guest room, but that was all we needed. We had each other and that was all we wanted. After a wonderful honeymoon we returned to Whitegate, Measham, home of Sheila' s parents. I was so thankful to God for them and for the gift of their daughter.

114

Sheila's parents

Sheila was blessed with wonderful parents - Ivy and John Howard (Jack) Thirlby. Ivy was born in 1892, the fourth of seven children. Their father, John Wilkinson, was a farmer in Stapenhill, Burton on Trent. There was no public transport in Burton at that time and he started the horse buses which were specially made for him in Derby. These continued till the coming of the trams and the 'horse-less carriages', as the first cars were called. Ivy remembered trying to ride her grandfather's 'penny-farthing' bike and falling off it. Her sister, Jessie, trained at The London Hospital as a nursing sister and served in the First World War in Salonica and through the London Blitz in the Second World War. Her two youngest brothers, Ernest and Edward, became vets, Edward having the honour of being elected President of the Veterinary Association in 1956. Ivy trained as a teacher at Stockwell College, London. She very much wanted to go to Russia to teach English and studied Russian with the Berlitz School of Languages. All the plans were made but at the last minute she was stopped from going because the 1914-18 war was imminent. This was a great disappointment to her. She taught in Southsea until she was called home to Stapenhill to nurse the members of her family who were stricken with the terrible flu epidemic of 1919.

Jack was born in Measham in 1894, the third child of six, After attending Ashby Grammar school, he joined his father's grocery business until he was called up during the First World War, when he served with the Royal Engineers in Salonica. He and Ivy had met earlier in 1914 and after Jack went out to Salonica, their courtship was carried on through letters, until he came home safely in 1919. They were married in 1921 and their only daughter Sheila was born in 1923.

Opa and Oma

Times were hard after the war. When his father retired, Jack managed to get a job travelling for Johnston's, a London firm of wholesale grocers. His travels took him once a month as far as Grantham, where one of his customers was none other than Mr Roberts, father of Margaret, who later became Prime Minister, Margaret Thatcher. It was several years after the war that he was on his travels in Derbyshire on the 11th of November and he describes what happened next:

"In those days the two minutes silence was very strictly observed. I was watching the time carefully and as the hour approached I was nearing the town of Ashbourne. Ahead of me I could see extensive road works and the men were just stopping work. This I thought was a good place to stop, so I drew up alongside of the men who were lining up at the side of the road. I got out of the car and stood beside them. As the hooters called out the exact moment, a hand took hold of mine and held it firmly until the end of the silence. Then, turning to me, the owner of the hand said "Its a long way from Salonica, Jack!" He was an old comrade of my days in the Royal Engineers".

That was a memorable moment for both of them.

When Sheila started school, Ivy would have liked to go back to teaching, but at that time married women were not allowed to. It was much later that she was able to do so and had various posts, including one at the local Catholic school - almost unheard of at that time for a Protestant. After a spell as Head of a village school, she taught until retirement age in the large Secondary Modern School in Ashby. Both Jack and Ivy were active members of Measham Methodist Church; Jack having been both steward and circuit steward. Both had a great concern for others and many folk in and around Measham had reason to be truly grateful for their help in many different ways. In her autobiography, Mrs Elsie Childs JP dedicated her book "A Thankful Heart" to "Mrs Ivy Thirlby and Dr. J. W. Hart, whose encouragement and practical help have followed me from my girlhood days". (The book includes a section about Ivy.) Jack was skilled in letter writing both serious and also highly amusing (a skill that our son Peter later inherited) and he was often to be found composing letters for people in some kind of difficulty. He used his car widely to ferry folk about, including the preachers who came to Measham on Sunday. The Thirlby home often provided hospitality for visiting ministers and preachers, including a certain Reverend Eric Challoner. Ivy was a great campaigner and when many houses in the village were hit by coal- mining subsidence (including their own), she took up the cudgels with the National Coal Board, whose compensation at that time was inadequate. She travelled to the House of Commons with two men from the village and she herself confronted Lord Robens, Chairman of the NCB. Her meeting with him after an unpromising start, because of her persistence, proved profitable. By now Jack and Ivy were grandparents and greatly loved the two boys John and Peter, who called them, Opa and Oma' (this is Dutch for grandpa and grandma). In

August 1973 we moved from Alderley Edge to Cheadle but our first months there were overshadowed by Jack's illness. Sheila made frequent visits to Ashby, where her parents now lived, and, on January 23rd 1974, Jack died aged seventy nine. Ivy managed on her own until September of that year and then came to live with us for nine years, until we retired to Alsager in August 1983. Finally, she went into a nursing home in Nantwich where she received the nursing care she needed and where she died peacefully at the age of ninety two on January 23rd exactly to the day eleven years after Jack.

Waterfoot

We came straight from our honeymoon to Waterfoot, in the Rawtenstall circuit. This is in the Rossendale Valley in Lancashire. Our house was No.178, Burnley Road and stood high above this busy road. To reach it we had to climb a flight of stone steps. I had been used to the country and here we were in a densely populated area. Within a radius of a few hundred yards there were twelve places of worship, including three Methodist. My main church was Bethesda, a huge place with a gallery and a large hall below. Running past the church was the river Irwell and, alongside the river, were rows of houses, some perilously near to it. We had three happy years there. The most memorable was the year that our first child John was born. Sheila's first pregnancy had tragically ended in a miscarriage and this had been a great disappointment to us. However on 9th August 1952 John was born in the Rossendale General hospital, a fortnight before he was expected. I had left Sheila in the hospital on the Saturday evening and phoned early Sunday morning to know how she was. When the nurse told me that I had a son, I was overjoyed and felt like waking everyone on the terrace and telling them the good news. We had both independently chosen the same name

The Bethesda float at Waterfoot

John, after his grandfather John Howard Thirlby, John the Baptist and John Wesley, all good men and true. It was one of the proudest moments of my life when I held our baby son in my arms for the first time.

STORIES FROM THE VALLEY

Sarah Higginbotham

While I have been trying to relive those days I have been remembering some remarkable people and events. If ever I'm tempted to feel sorry for myself I think about this very remarkable lady who lived alone. She was totally blind and totally deaf. To get in I was told that I would need to go next door, to Mary, who not only had a key, but also had learnt how to communicate with Sarah using hand language. We went in and found her sitting at the side of a table and facing a warm coal fire. She had a bright shiny face and wore a white pinafore over her dress. She was used to Mary coming and going, but this time she recognised that Mary was not alone. With a real Lancashire accent she asked "Who's tha got with thee Mary?" Mary went to her and got hold of her hand and signalled that she had got the young parson. "Let's have a look at thee" she said, turning her face towards where I was standing. Mary asked me to kneel in front of her and she gently ran her fingers over my head and face, then round my clerical collar. She then put her hands together and said "Parson, say a prayer for me". I didn't find it easy to pray for a person who lived in a world of total darkness and silence. I prayed slowly and paused after each sentence. I was fascinated as Mary translated my prayer into a language that she could understand, through her fingers. The thing that I have remembered most clearly of that visit was Sarah's last word to me "Parson, will you also thank the Lord for all his goodness to me?"

The perfect demonstration

Waterfoot was a very busy place with its cotton mill, felt works and slipper factories. One of the felt workers who was a member of the church lost a finger at work. Some weeks later, when he was back at his job, the health and safety officer visited the place and asked him to explain just what had happened. He did more than explain, he gave a demonstration and in so doing lost another finger! When I was told this I didn't believe it and had to see the man with two fingers missing before I did. This surely was an occasion when truth was stranger than fiction.

The story of a sausage

I have met many interesting characters and witnessed strange things happening in my time, but none more so than this. It happened to a member of one of my churches. She took a leading part in the activities of the church and as far as I could judge, there was nothing abnormal about her at all. Then I had a phone call from her daughter, who was greatly distressed and very concerned about her mother who had been taken into the psychiatric hospital at Crumpsall. She didn't tell me what was the matter with her, but said that her mother would be very glad to see me. I went the next morning and found her in a large open ward, together with about twenty other patients. I was allowed to talk to her in the guest room. As soon as we were alone and seated Mrs 'A' said to me "Mr Challoner, it's good of you to come, I did so want to talk to you, for something very strange has happened to me. I've become a sausage". I just stared at her and said "A sausage!?" "Yes", she replied "and my daughter doesn't believe me. You believe me, don't you, Mr Challoner?" "Well", I said, "I know that you wouldn't tell me a lie, but I've never met anyone who had become a sausage before, tell me more". Stretching out her bare arm, she said "If you were to cut my arm you would discover that there is no blood there, just sausage meat." She spoke in such a natural, matter of fact way and obviously believed what she was saying and also seemed quite happy. So, I told her that I was glad that she was happy and said a prayer, asking God to bless her and to help her daughter to understand. We then went back into the open ward and she thanked me for being so understanding. I went to have a word with the chief nursing officer, feeling totally bewildered. This was a new experience for me and I found it hard to accept. He was used to it and said it was the result of a psychiatric illness which caused the patient to have very realistic delusions. Pointing to a chap who was sitting down and reading his paper he said, "That fellow thinks that he's a poached egg on toast and the one who is being a bit of nuisance, imagines he is laying a carpet and is now unrolling it and getting people to move out of his way.

The one who is standing on the chair and looking through the closed window down into the yard, thinks that he's Richard Dimbleby and is giving a running commentary on an imaginary royal procession". I must say that I found it all very puzzling, but also very interesting. I felt I had entered the world of Alice in Wonderland. Mrs A had gone into hospital in September and was there for five months. I brought her home in February. When I next visited her she had forgotten all about being a sausage and the matter was never mentioned again and as far as I know, no one in the church knew anything other than that she had suffered a nervous breakdown.

"Me Mam's on fire"

One of my churches was Hareholme and the leading lady there was Emma, wife of the local blacksmith, Fred Edge. They were a very interesting couple. On my first visit to Emma we were just having a chat in her front room, when suddenly there was such a noise coming from next door. We could hear banging and screaming and a boy of about seven came shouting "Me mam's on fire, me mam's on fire!" I rushed round and as I did so, I had to run under a line of washing. I grabbed a big towel and ran with it into the house and there this poor woman was beating her blazing frock with her bare hands. Her hair was burning too. I put the towel over her head and managed to lay her on the floor and put out the flames. Mrs Edge had sent for the ambulance and she was taken into hospital. Her burns were severe, but after several weeks she recovered and her hair began to grow but her face was scarred. It seems that when she went to light the gas oven with a match, the tap on the grill had been turned on. There was a bang and a ball of fire enveloped her.

Fred Edge and his wife became good friends and every time he met me his first greeting was "How's thee faither?" I had told him that father was a farmer and very interested in horses and how he had taught me as a lad of sixteen, to handle them. Fred loved horses and was fascinated to discover that their young parson could milk a cow by hand and plough a field with a team of horses. He was thrilled to join us when I arranged a coach outing to the New Pale, the 'home of the plough'.

Percy Richardson

Percy was the local cobbler. He was more, he was the local philosopher and friend to all. His shop was a meeting place, for all who called in for a chat and he had a low bench on which children would sit and talk to him on their way home from school. Before they left he would give each of them a sweet. People went to Percy's place, not only to have shoes mended but hurts healed also. When he was not cobbling, he would go climbing some of the hills that formed the Rossendale valley. His favourite was Seat Naze, which towered above the valley. Percy lived with his wife, who was severely disabled and looked after her.

It was noon, when he came down to the bus stop below our house, dressed in his Sunday suit. He was on his way to a friend's funeral. As he waited, he had a severe heart attack. An ambulance was called, but he was dead before they could get him to hospital.

Dear Percy! The question on everyone's lips was "What's going to happen to his wife now; and who's going to tell her?" They asked me if I would do it! I dreaded the idea, but went. The sun was shining, but it was a very black day for us all. The door was never locked and I knocked and walked straight in. She greeted me with the words "If you've come to see Percy, you'll be disappointed, he's gone to a funeral". I said that I had in fact come to see her. She sensed that something was the matter and thought that I wasn't well. I told her "I'm afraid that I've got some bad news. Percy has had an accident and has been taken to hospital." It wasn't the whole truth, but I thought putting it like this might cushion the shock. It didn't. She panicked and cried out, "How did it happen? Is it very serious? Will he be all right?" I realised that I had made a bad mistake in going on my own. I ought to have taken with me her neighbour who was a close friend. So I went for her and together we told her that Percy had died. She just wouldn't believe it and kept crying "No, not our Percy, not our Percy."

A mountain-top experience with a difference

The whole community was shocked, and the church was packed for his funeral. His will stated that when he died he wanted his ashes to be scattered on the top of Seat Naze! So on a Sunday afternoon some days after the funeral, a party of close friends gathered together and made a pilgrimage to the top of Seat Naze. The undertaker carried the ashes and led the way. It was a steep climb to the top and when we arrived the undertaker, now very breathless, asked us to stand in a semicircle with our backs to the wind so that when the ashes were scattered the wind would take them away from us. After a short reading and prayer, his ashes were scattered and we returned to the valley below.

Percy was a good man who had cobbled shoes to the glory of God.

Should I have been a monk?

There are those who advocate a celibate ministry. Looking back on my life, the sort of ministry that I practised, especially in the early days, was more suitable for a single man than one who was married. I have already said that the two years that I had at Measham were probably the most fruitful. Then I was single. I couldn't have done all the things that I did if I had been married with a family. However, when I was married and had a family I tried to do the same. My engagement diaries for those early years, showed that I seldom had a day off and had meetings almost every evening.

The Minister's Sabbath

Today it's the custom for all ministers to have one day each week free. This is the minister's Sabbath. At no time in my ministry did I have a fixed day off. I tried to keep Saturdays free, but in practice there would be weddings, etc, which swallowed my Saturday up. The result of all this - I confess - is that I've neglected my wife and two boys. Sheila has never complained, except when she felt that I was doing too much and needed a break for my own sake. When she read my self-criticism above, she wanted me to cut it out. But I know that it's true and I leave it in because it might be a warning to some younger minister who might happen to read this.

Two good lads in spite of . . .

As the boys grew up I did try to have some time with them on Saturday mornings, but we were very restricted in what we could do then. I rarely took them to a football match and in spite of having been a Scoutmaster I missed the opportunity of going camping with them. It was only when they were older that we had camping holidays as a family. As every parent soon learns, children grow up so very quickly. They go to school, college or university and leave home and before we realise it, have become almost strangers. Our sons have been fortunate in that they have had a good mother, who has always been thoughtful, understanding and generous to them. In spite of my failings they have been good lads, done well at school and both managed to get an Honours degree at University. Many parents would envy us. But I wish that we had done more things together when they were younger. If I had my time over again, instead of the family having the 'left-overs' of my time, I would reserve some prime time for them. Sometimes when I thought family commitments were interfering with my work, I would say to Sheila, "I think I ought to have been a monk". Her reply was, "You're too much of a monkey to be a monk!" She was probably right - as usual.

CHAPTER TEN

THE NEW MANSE AT ASTON, NEAR NANTWICH

God moves in a mysterious way;
His wonders to perform.
William Cowper.

I've been very fortunate in my ministry in the colleagues that I've had and without exception I can say that they have all been friends, as well as colleagues. That didn't mean that we always agreed, but if necessary agreed to differ. The day we moved into the Rossendale Valley, the Superintendent minister, Ernest Foster, also moved into the circuit with his family and for three years we were colleagues there. Whilst I had been happy and very reluctant to leave my 'Super', my invitation as a probationer minister had been for three years and I was anxious to get back into the country and to be nearer home. So when a well known Cheshire farmer, Mr Lea Mulliner, 'phoned, asking if I would be interested in coming as second minister to live in a new manse at Aston, near Nantwich, I told him that I was very interested. This was an area that I knew well, for it was quite near to Reaseheath Agricultural College and within easy reach of my parents. Sheila and I and baby John went and saw the churches and the manse - which was only partly built at that time - and met some of the officials. Two days later we received by post a formal invitation which we gladly accepted.

Tragedy strikes at the manse
Some time later tragedy struck the Foster family. Their eldest daughter had recently married a young electrical engineer who was engaged in important research work. An experiment had gone wrong, causing an explosion which killed him. The manse where they lived overlooked the church graveyard and following this tragedy they found it a very depressing outlook and decided they must move. It was just at this time that I went over to Aston to see how the manse building was progressing and met the builder, Bill Garnett, who was also a circuit steward. As we talked together he told me that the previous evening their 'Super' surprised everybody by informing them that he wanted to leave and they were now looking for a replacement. I told them about Ernest Foster and suggested that he might be interested. He was; so for the second time, the Fosters and Challoners moved together, which I suppose is a rare happening. We were

Relaxing outside the new manse at Aston

sad about the reason for the Fosters leaving but very happy to have him as a colleague for another spell.

The church they wanted to close

Just before we moved, I had a letter from Frank Scott - the man whom I would be replacing - informing me that one of the churches in my section was scheduled to be closed, but a request had been made by a member of that church, Rupert Lee, that the closure be postponed until after the new minister had taken over. Frank Scott couldn't see any hope for this church as sometimes the congregation had been down to just one or two, but at my request they agreed to postpone the closure.

Rupert Lee, a man of faith

We discovered on arrival that the only person who saw any real hope for this little chapel was Rupert Lee himself. He was a most interesting fellow. Many thought him eccentric, which I suppose he was, but I found him to be very sincere and a man of faith and prayer. He lived only about fifty yards from the manse in The Cooperage, a bungalow he had built himself after retiring from the local garage. He had lived alone since his wife had died. Sheila was very kind to him, inviting him for his lunch every Monday and for many cups of coffee during the week. Soon after our arrival we started a weekly prayer meeting at the manse and Rupert never missed. He would pray passionately for the little chapel at Dodsgreen(the one scheduled to be closed) asking that God would make it a 'Temple of Youth'. All the previous ministers had lived in Whitchurch some six miles away, so I was in a much better position to see the local situation and to visit the few folk interested in the little chapel. This encouraged Rupert. He had a very old car, a big open tourer and on Sunday afternoons he would go collecting boys and girls from all round the district. One Sunday afternoon he

124

wasn't well and asked if I would collect the children, in his car, as mine wouldn't hold them all. When I agreed he told me where to pick up the first scholar (Bob), who would then guide me to where all the others lived.

Another less glorious chariot

Having being a farmer, I've been used to driving lots of farm vehicles, tractors etc. and an old war time jeep, but I had never driven anything like Rupert's 'Chariot'. The steering was so loose that it had to be turned half a circle before it made any difference. It was quite frightening at first, but when I got into the swing of it, I managed. Bob, who was directing me around Rupert's catchment area kept taking me further afield. After collecting seven, I suggested that was all we could manage, but young Bob exclaimed, "There are four more yet and Mr Lee always gets them in." I was thankful to arrive safely at the chapel and it was good to see the sheer joy of those children, but I was also thankful that no police car had come near; there weren't so many about then.

Rupert retires to Woodhall Spa

Rupert managed to carry on for a while, but the day came when he could no longer look after himself. He was offered and accepted, a place at the Home for Local Preachers at Woodhall Spa. I borrowed a Land Rover and horse-box from a farmer friend, Frank Huntbach, and took Rupert and his worldly goods to the Home. Folk thought that when he left, that would be the end of Dodsgreen, but by this time the congregation had been built up with the help of Fred and Leslie Fox and others. When I left Rupert at Woodhall Spa, it was a sad day for us and particularly for little John, for he loved 'Mitt Lee'. We still have one or two letters that he wrote to him after he had left, always signing himself 'EEL TREPUR' and leaving us and John to sort out why. He promised to keep praying for Dodsgreen chapel and asked me to send him the Preachers' plan so that he would know, each Sunday, who would be conducting the services there. On his wall he had a map of the area, which he had drawn himself, not only showing the houses, but also the names of the people for whom he prayed. He still had his vision of a 'Temple of Youth'. Would it ever come about?

A 'Temple of Youth?'

IT SO HAPPENED at that time that the headmaster of the local Church of England school had retired and his successor was to be a Mr Rodney Townsend, who had a family of four. His appointment was for the beginning of September and in the August, he, with his family, went on holiday to Barmouth, where there was a Children's Sand Mission each day and all the Townsend children went. I suppose you would say that Rodney at that time was a 'nominal Christian', attending church occasionally.

One morning *IT SO HAPPENED* that it was too wet to go on the sands and the children had to meet in a church hall and Rodney accompanied them. That

Trekkers Norman Smith and Alan Pringle talking to Eric's son John

morning, it wasn't only the children who were challenged, but he was too, and before the end of the holiday made a personal commitment to Christ. The family all moved into the school-house that August and Rodney, looking for some Christian Fellowship, came to see me. I told him about Rupert and his hopes for Dodsgreen and he was most interested. His wife, Alma, became the Sunday School Superintendent and their four children joined. I arranged for two young men to come from Cliff College for a ten day mission. Rodney was keen for the young people in the school to share in it and arranged for the young men to visit the school.

Another Mary

In preparation for the Cliff Mission I had leaflets printed and distributed and I also took it upon myself to find people who would provide meals for the men. I had intended going only to the homes of people who were already involved in some way in the life of the church. However, *IT SO HAPPENED* that as I was visiting one morning I saw a woman in her garden and felt led to have a word with her. I had, in fact, heard of her and knew her name was Mary Webster. She was a colourful character and her language too was often very colourful . . .

Although she lived near the chapel, she didn't attend any of the services and was very surprised when I called on her. She was even more surprised when I told her about the two young men who were coming and asked if she would be willing to give them their lunch one day. "Me?" she asked, "You want me to provide lunch for two of your preachers?" She just couldn't believe it. What I didn't know was, before she was married she had been a cook and when she realised that I was serious, she said, "If you think they would be willing to come to a place like this, then you send them, but they'll have to take me as they find me." When folk from the chapel heard what I had done; they were shocked. "Whatever will they think of us sending them to a place like that?"

Christ enters Mary's home and life

After they had been, the leader, Norman Smith, told me that she had produced a wonderful meal - a whole leg of lamb with all the trimmings - and he had got on well with her. Each time he came to the chapel he would pop in and she made him welcome. He asked several of us to pray especially for Mary. She had never mixed with the chapel folk and had no intention of doing so, but things began to happen in her life which were not of our doing. She came to a meeting and told everyone how, when alone in her bedroom, she had seen a light and felt a presence and had such a deep sense of guilt about her way of life that she got out of bed, fell on her knees, prayed for forgiveness and asked Christ to come into her life. Without her saying anything, it was quite obvious that she was a different woman. After the mission was over, Mary asked if she could look after the little chapel. We were happy for her to do this and she did it well. The first time that I preached there after the mission, Mary was sitting on the front row and seemed to be hanging on my every word. Amongst other things, I said that if we wanted God to continue to bless us as a church, then we must have a regular meeting for prayer. As soon as I had pronounced the benediction she got up and asked - so that everyone could hear her – "Mr Challoner, is it true that if we want God to continue to bless us we must have a regular meeting for prayer?". I said that it was. She then turned round and faced the congregation and asked them one by one if they wanted God to bless us. They all agreed that they did. "Then we had better have a regular prayer meeting" said Mary. "What do we have to do to start one?" I replied "Well, think of a day and time most convenient and meet". Mary then asked "What about next Friday?" No one objected, so Friday was fixed. .

Mary brings a new fire into the church

I couldn't manage the first meeting, but when I enquired, I learnt that eight had attended and Mary had led it. I did go to the second one and went early. Mary was already there standing in the doorway ready to greet me with a broad smile on her face and I felt that she had 'something up her sleeve'. She had! When I went into the school-room it had been transformed. Instead of the old broken fire grate which we didn't use, there was a lovely new grate and a warm fire burning. "Mary", I gasped, "where did this come from?" She replied, "Mr Challoner, if you ask no questions you'll be told no lies". "But Mary", I said, "I must ask, for it's the job of the Trustees to authorise and deal with such matters". Mary didn't know what Trustees were. She said "I've never seen any of them knocking about and as I was cleaning, I felt ashamed of that rusty old grate. I wouldn't have it even in my house and felt it wasn't right to have it in God's house. So when I got home I told our Jack (her husband) to go to Nantwich and buy another one and fix it, before the next prayer meeting. So if them there Trustees want to blame anyone, they must blame me". No one did blame her. Preachers who came to Dodsgreen were impressed with the new spirit of hope they found there and the growing congregation, especially the number of young people who now came. Mrs Townsend recruited more scholars and teachers. We, of course, kept Rupert Lee informed, but by this time he was very weak and died soon after. But the vision that he had was slowly becoming a reality – 'A Temple of Youth'.

P. S. We moved on from Aston to Alsager and during my second year in Alsager I was invited to go back to Dodsgreen, to conduct the OPENING OF THE EXTENSION TO THE CHURCH, WHICH WAS NEEDED TO HOUSE THE YOUTH WORK. I'm sure there would be rejoicing in heaven that day. There were tears of joy and tears of sadness, because Rupert was not there - at least not in the flesh. Dear old "Eel Trepur". His vision of a TEMPLE OF YOUTH had, in fact, become a reality.

Bilingual commando campaign

One of the highlights of my ministry at that period was the bilingual Commando Campaign around Flint. There was a team of about twenty ministers from English and Welsh Methodist Churches, working together under the leadership of Ron Marshall who had been in college with me. Several things stand out in my memory. As I was about to get into the car John, who was three, clung to me and didn't want to let me go. He cried "Daddy, daddy, you will come back, won't you?" As I travelled on to Flint his words kept ringing in my ears and I thought of the pain that so many little ones must feel when a marriage breaks up and daddy doesn't come back.

Another memory concerns something that happened at my first assignment. When visiting a Technical College, I asked to see the leader of the Christian Union and was directed to the Art Department. There, lying on a couch, which was on a raised platform was a young woman in the nude. About twenty art students with pads and pencils, were all drawing - at least until I went in. I apologised for bursting in on them but the model seemed unperturbed. I then explained that I was looking for the leader of the Christian Union and was introduced to Margaret. She arranged for me to have lunch in the dining hall, where I was able to speak to the students about the Campaign. When I told my story to the rest of the team some of the fellows were wanting to enrol for the Art class!

Facing the 'burning fiery furnace'

Another memory is our visit to the famous Shotton steel works. We were told to wear protective clothing. The, only protective clothing that I had was a long plastic mac, but when they opened the door of the huge furnace the heat was so intense that it melted my mac and the buttons 'ran down'. The men who worked in those conditions all day earned the admiration of all of us. Afterwards the account in the Methodist Recorder described it as a most memorable Campaign and stated that "Members of the team, one after another, had testified to having received a new vision, as they saw the power of the Gospel demonstrated, when young and old found faith in Christ."

I've got news for you. .

Soon after I got home from Flint, Sheila announced "I've got news for you, I think I'm pregnant." This was wonderful news, but after her previous miscarriage we were a little anxious. As the weeks went by our hopes were built up. However she had a setback and the doctor sent her into hospital for a few weeks. She managed to get over this crisis and came home, but had to spend much time in bed. We thought that all was well when she felt the baby move. But after a few more weeks our hopes were shattered and we lost our baby. It is difficult to describe our feelings as we wept together. Words from the Bible (significantly altered) came into my mind, "The Lord gave and the Lord has allowed to be taken away, blessed be the name of the Lord."

It was a Saturday when this happened, and months before I had arranged for a Circuit Youth Rally to be held on that night and had invited Ernest Steele from Cliff College to be our guest speaker and to stay with us for the weekend. Ernest arrived about an hour after this tragedy happened. He was, of course, shocked, but he was a great comfort to us. I couldn't leave Sheila or little John, who had been playing next door with his friend 'big John' who was six. Ernest went to the meeting and explained the reason for my absence. They were all very upset and afterwards one of the older members of the Circuit Youth Fellowship, David Wright, came to the Manse as spokesman for the others. In my mind's eye I can see David now, standing at our front door, unwilling to come in, unable to speak. He took my hand, held it for a moment and then turned away and as he did so said "We're all very sorry." That gesture of love and sympathy meant more to us than David could ever know. We felt uplifted by the prayers of so many, by the messages that we received and were thankful for Sheila's mother, who came to look after us all for several weeks. But the loss hurt.

I've lived those days over again a number of times when I've tried to comfort young parents who had suffered the grievous loss of a child and also again as I've been writing this chapter in my life. John was a bright little lad and such a joy to us both and we longed for him to have a little sister or brother. We were encouraged when the doctor said, "I see no reason why you shouldn't" but I was

Left - Little John and Big John. Right - John (incognito) wearing Opa's hat.

very fearful of the possibility of Sheila having again to go through what she had already gone through and in the end be bereft of her child. We prayed much about this and finally got the assurance that it was right for us to try again. In just over a year, after a trouble free pregnancy, a bonny fair-haired little boy, Peter Eric, was born. We were thrilled and so thankful to God. John was delighted to have a little brother and so very proud of him.

I've got a mouse in my bed

During my ministry I have answered many urgent calls to the manse. One such call came to Aston. It was past midnight and Sheila and I were fast asleep when the 'phone rang. I hurried downstairs, picked it up and a voice cried out, "Mr Challoner, can you come?" I recognised the voice of an elderly lady and said "Mrs Adams, whatever's the matter?" Her reply was not funny, but I found it difficult not to laugh. "I've got a mouse in bed with me and it just ran over my feet." I told her that I'd come round at once, so I slipped my overalls over my pyjamas, jumped on my bicycle and went in pursuit of this little four-legged intruder. I was able to let myself in, ran upstairs into her bedroom and there sitting up in bed was this ninety year old lady. She apologised for calling me in the middle of the night and said "I didn't know who else to call". I suggested that I made a cup of tea and while I was waiting for the kettle to boil I looked round the pantry for a mouse trap. I found three in a cupboard and having seen mouse droppings on the pantry shelf I set one there, and then took our cups of tea upstairs. We sat and talked and I read to her part of Psalm 27, which ends with the words "Wait on the Lord, be of good courage and he shall strengthen thine heart." We then had a short prayer and I assured her that no little mouse would ever hurt her and that she could rest in peace. Just as I was about to leave, I heard a click downstairs. The trap had gone off and I had caught one. During the next few days I caught three more and Mrs Adams never shared her bed with another mouse. I did suggest that it might be a good idea for her to have a cat, but she thought it would be a bigger worry, even than the mice.

130

Another 'call'

It must have been about two years after the mouse incident, that I had another 'call'. This was very different, but no less dramatic. Some might question the nature of this call but I believe that it was a call from God in answer to a genuine cry for help. During my ministry I've had other similar calls, which confirm my belief that they were calls from God. It was a Friday morning. The time was eleven o'clock. I was sitting at my desk preparing my services for the following Sunday. Quite suddenly I knew that I had to go at once to see Mrs Adams. The call was urgent, I jumped on my bicycle and peddled as though her life depended on my getting there. I raced past the road-man who stared as I dropped my bike at Mrs Adams' gate. I ran up the garden path, to the back of the house, got the key and unlocked the back door. As I entered I heard her cry "Mr Challoner." She was lying on the floor in her dining room. She had fallen and bruised her face and was in a state of shock. She said "I cried out to the Lord and asked him to send you, I knew you would come."

IT SO HAPPENED that I was available at that time and that I not only recognised the 'call' but responded to it.

I gently pushed a cushion under her head and then 'phoned for the doctor, who came and examined her as she lay there. He could find no broken bone but she had banged her head and was badly bruised. Together we put her on the settee and he asked me to arrange for some one to look after her. Mrs Adams had no family and now had no close relatives left. I had often heard her speak of Mary from Alsager. This was her closest friend and she asked me to tell her what had happened. (When I made the call to Alsager that Friday morning, I never dreamt that one day I would be receiving a 'call' to go there as minister.) I got through to Mary - Mrs Millward - and told her what had happened. She was, of course, very upset and arranged for Mrs Adams to be brought to Milverton, her lovely home in Alsager, where she stayed for some time and where she eventually died.

The very amateur sweep

I enjoy mending things that are broken and restoring them and at one time I had at least half a dozen clocks in my bedroom at the New Pale; these, including a grandmother clock, had been given me to mend and I was usually successful. We now have a Grandfather clock - a family heirloom that has been handed on to the youngest son in the family - and on several occasions when it wouldn't go, I've managed to mend it. I enjoy doing a job myself if possible, rather than call in a professional and over the years must have saved hundreds of pounds. But sometimes things have gone wrong.

We had a lovely manse at Aston - in fact the best that we ever had. In the dining room there was a fire grate and in winter we were able to keep a fire going both night and day. When it began to smoke and needed sweeping, Rupert Lee said that he had rods and a brush if I could find anyone willing to do it. Now the grate

*John with his
baby brother
Peter*

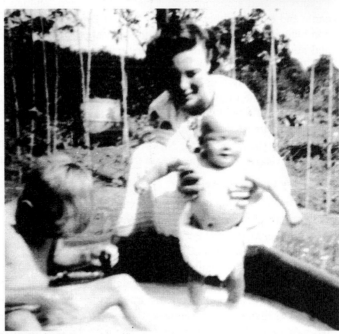

*Sheila, John
and Peter
"cooling off"*

backed on to the wall of the garage and in the garage there was a flu door, which meant that instead of having to push the rods up from the fire grate, they would go from the garage. This sounded to me to be something that I could do, so I

132

decided to have a go one Saturday afternoon while Sheila was shopping in Nantwich and I was left to look after John.

The day arrived for action. As soon as she had gone, I hurried across to Rupert's for his rods and brush. I blocked the front of the grate up with the tin shield that he had specially cut for me to use when I lit the fire. This was a good fit and ideal for the job and would prevent any soot from getting into the room! I had a big bag ready to receive the soot in the garage then screwed the brush on to the first rod and pushed it through the flu door. Then a second and third. I was surprised at the clouds of soot that came down, but instead of it coming out through the flu door into my bag in the garage, it fell into the grate. I went round into the dining room to see that all was well. Thankfully the tin was doing a good job, so back I went and continued pushing the brush higher as I screwed on more rods. Then when I thought I'd finished, something terrible happened. The weight of all the soot had been pressing hard on the tin in the front of the grate and had suddenly forced it out into the room. I rushed round and was met by John crying "Daddy, daddy". When I went into the room I saw a sight I never forgot, There was soot everywhere and I just stared in disbelief. I asked John to run across to ask Mrs Welch - 'big John's' mum - to come. She stood in the doorway of the dining room and just stared. "Whatever shall I do?" I asked. "If I were you I'd pack my bags and go before Sheila comes back" was her quick reply. We had almost two hours to try to clean up. She went home to change and quickly returned bringing her powerful industrial cleaner. We took the curtains down, shook them outside and hung them on the line and put the soot into bags. It was fortunate that it was a lovely day and we were able to put things on the lawn. The soot was dry and the vacuum cleaner did a good job. I kept looking anxiously at the clock, wondering whatever Sheila would say. When she did come she thought there had been a fire so her first reaction was one of relief. I'm glad that she didn't see it when the tin first fell. That was the first and last time that I ever attempted to sweep a chimney.

More trouble at the manse

This was not the only time that Sheila arrived back from Nantwich on a Saturday afternoon and discovered trouble at the manse. On another occasion I was looking after John and Peter, who was now able to walk. We were having a game with John playing the part of a cowboy, and I was his bucking bronco. Of course Peter wanted to play too and have a ride. I got on my hands and knees, placed my head between his legs and lifted him up on my neck. He was a chubby little lad and quite heavy for his age and it certainly didn't do my neck any good as he wriggled and kicked. It was at this moment that John, who was then a lively lad of six, jumped from a chair and landed on the middle of my back just as he had seen Roy Rogers do. My back seemed to give way under the impact and I collapsed on to the floor. I tried to get up but couldn't. Sheila arrived back soon afterwards and John ran to greet her with the words "Mummy, daddy has had an accident." By this time I'd managed to get up and was feeling better so we decided not to send for the doctor.

Important visitors come looking for a minister

The next morning I was preaching at Aston and although my back was very painful I decided to take the service. When I arrived at the church one of the stewards came to me and said that there were several distinguished looking visitors in the congregation. When I went up into the pulpit I saw them but I didn't know who they were or where they came from. The one thing that I did know was that I wasn't feeling well and my back was very painful. I managed the first half of the service, including the children's address, and then it was time for me to come down to receive the offering. One of the collectors was a little girl and as I reached down to take the plate from her I couldn't straighten my back. I managed to sit down on a chair and told the congregation that I couldn't carry on with the service. We sang the hymn that I had chosen; I then pronounced the benediction and walked bent almost double, out of the church. Sheila took me home in the car and I took no more services that day.

Two of the stewards came to see me and told me that the visitors were from the Sandbach and Alsager circuit and were looking for a minister for 1959. The visitors had been very concerned about me. Although they hadn't heard me preach a sermon, they must have been satisfied with what they had heard and what the congregation had said about me. It was on the strength of this that I was invited.

CHAPTER ELEVEN

70 STATION ROAD, ALSAGER,
STOKE- ON- TRENT

When I think of those who have influenced my life the most,
I think not of the great but of the good.

John Knox.

The visitors representing the Sandbach and Alsager Circuit who came to Aston to hear me preach recommended that I be invited to Alsager, in spite of the fact that I couldn't complete the service because of a back injury. So on August 27th 1959, we moved. The boys were sad to leave Aston, and after we had finished our evening meal on that first day, Peter asked, "Daddy, can we go home now?" I explained to him that this was his home now, but he argued and said, "I want to go back to my real home". However they both soon settled down, and accepted No. 70 as their new home.

John and Peter with Pongo

The manse at Alsager. Eric, Sheila, Peter and Pongo

Edna Weatherby taking a class in the school room at Wesley Place. Peter is third from the right.

When we arrived in Alsager the church had just said farewell to the Rev. Horace Ibbotson and his wife Lucy (affectionately known as Mrs Ibb). She was a wonderful lady and had a remarkable ministry in the church, especially amongst the young people (YPF). These young folk loved her, for through her ministry many of them had found a new purpose for living and they were sad when she left.

At first it was difficult for us living under the shadow of our predecessors. But I knew that back at Aston there were a lot of people who were missing both Sheila and me; and our successors would be having the same problem. It was no use worrying, we simply had to 'do our own thing' and build on the foundations that they had left.

Essence of cow patch and roses!

Recently I phoned Pat Peddie, (now the wife of Rev. Geoffrey Peddie) who was one of those who had been in this YPF. She spoke about Mrs Ibb, and talking to Pat reminded me of the following happening.

Having been a farmer, I knew the value of well-rotted farm yard manure for growing a good crop of vegetables and enriching all the soil in the garden. So when a local farmer, who was retiring from the farm asked if I'd like to have some good manure for my garden, I gladly accepted. However, he made a condition. If I had any, I had it all. He didn't want any left and he wanted it moved by the following Sunday. I agreed and said that I would come for it on Friday evening. I borrowed a tractor and trailer from another farmer who wanted it back on the Saturday afternoon; however, I seriously miscalculated just how much manure there was. I thought that I would have got it all on one big load, but failed, and it was dark, and I had no lights, so I decided to go before breakfast on Saturday morning. This I did, and was amazed to discover that I couldn't get it all on a second load and would need to return after breakfast.

You must be wondering just what all this has got to do with Pat and Geoffrey. It so happened that Saturday was their Wedding Day and I was due to officiate at 11.00 am.

At 10.30 I went roaring through the town with half a load of good farm-yard manure, and passed guests going to the wedding! One lady who saw me said to her husband as I went past, "Jack, that fellow on the tractor looked very much like Mr Challoner, but it couldn't have been for he's marrying Pat and Geoffrey." It was me and as I sped along Station Road, sweat running down my face, very hot and very dirty, I could see Sheila standing in the road looking anxious. I jumped off the tractor and ran up into the bathroom. Sheila had thoughtfully run the water and I quickly jumped in the bath.

After a very quick bath, I put on my wedding suit, but my hands still smelled of cow manure. Here I made a mistake (another one!). There was a small bottle of scent on the dressing table and not having ever used scent I decided that on this occasion it might be a good idea. I shook it on to my hands, rubbed it well in and for good measure put some on my neck. I arrived at the church at five minutes to eleven smelling like a perfumery. Pat arrived on time looking lovely. She didn't even notice the minister's very potent 'after shave'.

By the way, we had some wonderful crops of vegetables for years afterwards.

The 'Hello' girls

The manse in Station Road was just opposite the Telephone Exchange. It wasn't a digital exchange, so a number of 'Hello girls' (this is what we called them) were employed on the switchboard. I had an upstairs study and could see these girls when they came to their recreation room. One morning I had a number of important calls to make, but could not get through to the exchange. Each time that I tried it was engaged. I was so fed up that I dashed down stairs and across the road, in through the front entrance and into the switch board room. The supervisor happened to be one of our members from Wesley Place, and she could see that I was agitated, and hurried across to me. "Is something wrong, Mr Challoner?" she asked. I told her how long I had been trying to get a call through.

I could see the row of girls all busy working away and above each girl, on the top of her board, were a number of red lights. The supervisor pointed out that all the red lights indicated people waiting to get their calls through. I stood there for at least five minutes and couldn't believe my eyes. As they cleared the calls others came in, and they were kept busy pulling plugs out, and pushing plugs in, in a frantic effort to connect people. It made me feel quite dizzy just watching. I never complained again and became much more patient and understanding when I couldn't get through.

A Stanley Matthews fan.

I'd never gone regularly to a football match until we came to Alsager and there, Arthur Bailey organised a coach to all the Stoke City home matches. I started to attend when I was free from other engagements and enjoyed it very much, especially when Stanley Matthews was playing. But I had a problem. I'm not a passive watcher. I like to give vocal support to my team and at the end of an exciting match, I'd arrive home with very little voice and a few times found it difficult to make myself heard on Sunday.

A real crisis arose, when, after one particularly exciting game, I saw Stanley dribble his way almost from one end of the pitch to the other and then score. I shouted as loud as a Brazilian football commentator and threw my hat in the air in my excitement. I arrived home without either my hat or my voice. Sheila said "That's it! You'll either have to stop shouting or stop going". I stopped going. But on the Sunday morning following the match I could only speak in a whisper so, in desperation, Sheila 'phoned Dr. Bates who wasn't only our doctor, but he and his wife were our friends. Mrs Bates answered and when Sheila told her of my problem she said "Tell him to come to the house and I'll give him something for it". I went and she gave me *Sanderson's Specific*, telling me to gargle with it. I did and felt as though I'd gargled with paint stripper. It made my voice stronger, but I never took any more for the cure was worse than the complaint!

Can you give me a funeral service tonight?

It was Christmas Eve, it was snowing and almost midnight. The boys had gone to bed, we'd filled their stockings and I was putting the finishing touch to my services for Christmas day when the door-bell rang. I opened it and there standing (only just) was Sam (not his real name) looking very much the worse for drink. It was bitterly cold so I asked him to come in.

He was married, had two young boys and a good job. But Sam had a big drink problem and he knew that this was ruining his home and family life. Twice he had lost his job and twice - after much pleading from me - had it given back on condition that he 'kept off the bottle'. I should add that when he was sober, he was a really good fellow. I was very fond of him, and found it heart breaking to see him like this. But what followed next?

He sat on a chair, holding his head in his hands, then he looked up and said very slowly and quietly, "I know that I've had too much drink. I know that I've again let you down, but in spite of the drink, I know what I'm saying and I know what I'm doing and what I'm going to do". He was very serious at this point and I just wondered what he was going to say next. He went on "I've given a lot of thought to this and I've decided that it would be better for my wife and lads, better for my boss, better for you, and, in fact, better for every one if I were dead. I've made arrangements for taking my own life tonight, but before doing so I've come to ask of you a very special favour. Will you give to me a short funeral service; just a reading and a prayer committing my soul into the hands of God, and asking for forgiveness for me? Then I could die peacefully". I told Sam that this was a most unusual request and that I'd always been used to conducting a funeral service *after* a person had died, but never *before*. But I could see that he was serious and so I asked Sheila if she would make us each a cup of strong black coffee. When Sheila brought the coffee I asked her not to wait up as I would probably be some time before I came to bed.

We were still talking at 2.30 am by which time he'd sobered up and I had managed to convince him that suicide was not a good idea. Then he asked me if I would say a prayer asking for God's help. I said that I wouldn't pray for him until he had done three things:

1   Promised to seek professional help about how to overcome his drink problem.
2   Promised to apologise to his family, and ask for their forgiveness.
3   Promised to get rid of any drink that he had in the house.

He was hesitant about this last promise, for he'd stocked up for Christmas. But I was adamant. "You think about it, Sam, while I make another cup of coffee". I made the coffee and as he took his cup he said "I do promise but what will you do with all the drink?". "Leave that to me, Sam" I said. "but I can assure you when I've finished with it, it wont hurt anyone else in the way that you and yours have been hurt. "

A prayer after a promise.

With that we both knelt down by the side of the settee in our lounge and as I prayed he wept. Then I got up and dressed myself ready to face the cold winter night, and took him home in my car.

It was now 3.15 am on Christmas morning. Anyone seeing us both going into Sam's house at that hour would assume I was bringing him back from a pre-Christmas party - what a party.

I had put a cardboard box for the bottles in the boot of my car and followed Sam into his pantry with it. He handed me the bottles without protesting. Then I staggered to the car with them, and hurried home to bed. I think Sheila thought I had been 'playing Father Christmas'. I suppose, in a way, I had.

The problem of getting rid of the drink

I hadn't been in bed very long before I was awakened by two little lads giving cries of delight as they discovered that Father Christmas had been. As they searched for the hidden mysteries in their stockings, I thought of the two little lads who might never have seen their Father Christmas again.

After a quick breakfast I hurried off to take my first service at 9.30 am and another at 10.30, then back home to change ready for our journey to Sheila's parents, where we would be having our Christmas celebrations and staying for a few days. Sheila had been busy getting the cases packed and the boys ready after taking them to the 9.30 service. I was about to go out to put these cases in the boot of the car, when I realised that I hadn't dealt with the drink. I told Sheila to come and have a look. She was horrified. " Whatever in the world are you going to do with all that stuff?" she asked. My reply was "I'm going to make a cocktail that will do no one any harm".

I took the box in the garden shed, opened the bottles one by one, and emptied the contents of each into a big bucket, and then emptied this down the drain. Our garden shed smelled like a beer tavern. Then I started to put the bottles into our dustbin. Sheila came out and saw me. "You can't put all those bottles in our dust bin" she cried. "Well, what shall I do?" I asked. "Put them in the boot, and we'll leave them in a lay-by refuse bin" she replied. I put all the empty bottles in the boot as requested. This now made the car smell.

Caught in the act.

I never realised how difficult it was going to be to dispose of those smelly bottles. In fact we had gone beyond Burton-on-Trent, the beer town, and had almost reached Measham before we stopped. I lifted the boot and began throwing the bottles into a wire waste-basket. As I did so, a car went past, and the driver, seeing what we were doing, gave a knowing toot on his car horn, as much as to say "I caught you". We had some explaining to do when we reached Sheila's parent's home, but we all had a wonderful Christmas.

Sam did, in fact, overcome his drink problem after a very valiant effort. He got another job, and became a caring father, a good husband, and a workman who was trusted.

A very important event in the life of the church.

Writing in the May issue of our Monthly Messenger 1962 I forecast that a Christian Stewardship Campaign would prove to be a very important event in the life of the church. That forecast was correct. Looking back some thirty five years later, I would say that it was one of the most important events of my ministry.

The climax of that Campaign was the Church dinner - but more about that later.

When we launched out, we faced much criticism. Folk said, "It is just a gimmick to get more money". We certainly needed more money, but this wasn't our main aim - simply a by-product.

Having been minister at Wesley Place for almost three years I was able to assess our fundamental need as a church. There was a need for us to rethink our relationship with God, as regards our TIME, TALENTS and TREASURE.

I wrote to the Methodist Stewardship HQ in London and they arranged for a Mr Cherry to come to guide us through the campaign and to instruct the Hostesses and Visitors in all they had to do. This relieved me of a great burden. He was first class.

A super dinner for all - free!

He knew that the big question was "How do we get people to come together to discuss personal matters, especially when they think it's their money that we're after?" The answer was - said Mr Cherry - a super Church dinner, to which each person on our Church Roll was invited. We decided in faith to go ahead with the idea.

Having studied the Church Family Roll, he suggested that we ought to think in terms of catering for 260. It wasn't easy to find a place large enough for so many. In the end we booked the Queens Hall in Burslem with caterers to provide dinner free for every one. 248 attended the dinner. The hostesses each looked out for those they had invited and showed them to their places. It was an excellent meal and the friendly relaxed atmosphere prepared the way for the speeches, none of which were long. Two people gave a word of testimony telling what the church meant to them. I had a word and explained that each guest would receive a brochure which had been especially prepared, outlining the aim of the Campaign including pictures illustrating the life and work of our church.

Then I announced that we had appointed twenty Visitors and that each person would receive a call from one of these, who would discuss with them the contents of the brochure. Here are a few of the statistics resulting from the Campaign.

250 Homes were visited.

240 Time and Talent forms were filled in.

199 Boxes of Offering Envelopes were issued.

14 Joined a Confirmation class.

27 Received Daily Bible Reading Notes.

19 Asked for a visit from the minister.

21 Asked for information about Younger Wives.

26 Asked for information about Men's Fellowship.

23 Asked for information about Wesley Guild.

16 Offered to help in the Sunday School.

11 Offered to help in the choir.

18 Offered to provide transport in their car.

14 Offered to help in maintenance of church building and grounds.

19 Offered to visit the sick and elderly.

16 Offered to do Secretarial work.

17 Offered their special qualifications.

This was most encouraging, but it did give us a real challenge to find jobs for all these volunteers. Our congregations increased and our weekly offerings were almost doubled. A very lively Men's Fellowship was formed which we called Koinonia.

Jim didn't fix it but Lewis did

We invited those who offered to help in the maintenance of church buildings and grounds to a meeting to consider how best we could use them.

At that time we were in need of more space to park cars. There was some rough ground to the left of the church which needed levelling and covering with hard core. This would make a good car park. Several offered to help with this but we needed two things; a machine and a driver, and some hard core. One of the men said that if we could level the ground he would provide the hard core.

IT SO HAPPENED that at the Sunday School Anniversary at Rode Heath, in my address to the children I'd been talking about Jimmy Saville, who used to invite people to write to him to tell him what they would like to do and he would try to fix it for them. I said if I wrote to him I would like him to fix it for me to drive a powerful bulldozer. After the service, I had tea with the Sunday School superintendent, Mr Lewis Price and his wife Marjorie. Now *IT SO HAPPENED* that Lewis was head of a firm of builders which had a number of bulldozers and he had said that he could fix it for me to drive one. I told the maintenance people about Lewis's offer and said if they wished I would do the levelling. One member

A greeting on the steps at Wesley Place

said, "Are you sure that you won't level the church at the same time?" I assured him that I wouldn't and they agreed that I ask Lewis to 'fix it'. Lewis arranged for a man to bring one of his smaller machines on a low loader and leave it at the church one afternoon then I could have the use of it just for one night and it would be collected the next day at 7 am.

We agreed on the date. I arranged for several of the maintenance men to come with spades and rakes that night at 7 pm. I was at the church well before 4 pm waiting - not without some trepidation - for the machine to arrive. Although I'd been a Land Army Instructor in the war and had a good knowledge of tractors, I had no experience of these earthmoving machines. Lewis' s man arrived on time, quickly unloaded it and said his instructions were to give me what help I needed before he left. This he did, and I was glad of it.

Although it was classed as a small machine, it was much longer than I anticipated, having a pusher at the back as well as the front, and I had to be very careful when swinging round. However by the time my helpers had arrived I was getting a little bit of confidence and began to show off my 'skills'. On one side was the church building, and on the other a wall separating the yard from a row of houses whose backs overlooked us. This was an old wall and I knew if I touched it, there was a real danger of it falling down, so I had to go carefully. This was one of the occasions when I wished that I had an extra pair of eyes at the back of my head.

The minister leaves his mark on the Church.

I knew that we couldn't finish before it was dark so I'd arranged for us to have some powerful lights to enable us to keep going in the dark. The longer I worked the more confident I got - in fact too confident. I was most careful when working near the wall but once, while watching my front as I levelled off towards this wall, I reversed and at the same time swung round. There was a shuddering bang. I'd hit one of the main buttresses of the church with my back pusher. The whole machine shook, and so did the driver. I jumped off and was so thankful to see only a small piece had been broken out of a brick. I jumped back on to the machine, and anxiously tried to see if I could still lift and drop the back pusher. I could, so all was well. It was time to switch on the lights but it was also time for us have a break. My team had been working hard and so had I. So when someone suggested bringing fish and chips we happily accepted

When I borrowed this bulldozer, I overlooked the fact that it had a governor on it which automatically opened up the throttle when it was pushing hard. There was very little - if any - silencing on the exhaust which meant that at every 'push' it sounded as though a jet plane was setting off from our church car park and the roar echoed round the houses and the church.

About half past eleven a very angry neighbour shouted from his bedroom window. He let us know that he wasn't able to sleep, neither could 'half of Alsager' and if we didn't stop he would 'phone the police. I felt very guilty about this, apologised to him and stopped at once. Fortunately I had by this time levelled most of the ground and we were able to finish the whole job by hand, including laying the hard core.

So a job that would have cost the church several hundred pounds cost nothing but a few anxious moments and a lot of hard work and another outcome of the Christian Stewardship Campaign was a new car park and the minister discovering a hidden talent.

The new vicar comes round on his bike.

It would make an interesting exercise to go through this book and examine the number of times when the ringing of a bell, a door bell or telephone bell, has heralded an exciting adventure or the beginning of a new and interesting relationship. This story is about the latter.

The telephone rang one Monday morning and the voice of a stranger enquired "Is that the Methodist minister?". I replied that it was. He said "I'm John Stopford and I've just taken up my appointment here in Alsager as the vicar of St Mary's. I'm ringing because our Bishop has asked me to make contact with the local Methodist minister and to discuss with him the business of Anglican-Methodist Conversations. I've just returned from missionary work abroad and haven't been involved in these Conversations and I wondered what your thoughts were on this matter". I told him that I was much more interested in discussing what our two churches could do together for the people of Alsager.

His reply was "Thank God for that, can I come round to talk to you?" I suggested that he came at once and had a coffee with me, which he did. At once I felt that here was a kindred spirit, a man I could talk to, and a man I could pray with. We didn't need any 'Conversations'.

What we did do was to discuss together the idea of preparing a project in which both churches could be involved. We decided on a house-to-house visitation campaign at Linley (a housing estate on the outskirts of the town), based at St Luke's Church, Linley - a daughter church of St Mary' s.

We would go out in couples, Methodist and Anglican together, and would meet in St Luke's for prayer. Couples would be given a notebook on which to write the details of each visit and the response. Two people from each church would be asked to prepare light refreshments for all the team after visits.

The Campaign was well received and proved a great success and resulted in the formation of a Mother and Toddler group and a united service occasionally. But for me the most important result was that John and I became good friends and a new understanding resulted between the two churches.

I'm writing these notes at the end of 1997, just thirty five years after the Linley Campaign. Last Sunday I was invited to speak at an ecumenical service at St. Mary' s on the subject of 'Looking Back'. I told of my own personal experience, and how my attitude to other denominations had changed over the years. Here is an extract from that address on October 12th 1997:

One of the biggest stumbling blocks to unity and peace in the world is religion and religious people. No-one who has studied history can deny this and no-one who looks round the world today can deny it either. Tonight I've been asked to look back.

When I began my ministry I was a fundamentalist. I'm now, but my fundamentals are different.

I was quite clear in my mind then that I knew what was right and what was wrong. I was also clear who was right and who was wrong. That made life less complicated. There were only two groups to deal with. Those who were right and those who were wrong.

I believed then that Roman Catholics were wrong because they prayed to the Virgin Mary. I could find no evidence in my Bible to justify this. I thought then that high Anglicans were wrong because they dressed up like Roman Catholic priests, burned incense, and bowed to a wooden cross. I could find no evidence in my Bible to justify this. What's more, I believed that one of our leading Methodists, Dr Leslie Weatherhead was a heretic! I'd heard that he had questioned the Virgin Birth of Christ!

Imagine my horror when I went to the Ministerial Training college in Birmingham and learnt that the guest speaker in our first special service was none other than Dr Leslie Weatherhead.

I decided to boycott the service, but was persuaded not to, by my close friend, Roy Dew. However I warned him that if Dr. Weatherhead said anything heretical I would openly protest.

All the students were assembled, and stood as the Principal, Dr. W. Howard, followed by Dr. Weatherhead walked slowly down the aisle. Dr. Weatherhead was dressed like a Roman Catholic Priest. He stopped before the cross and bowed low, and then sat down. I was ready to leave before he'd said a word, but Roy had positioned himself at the end of the pew, and didn't leave room for me to pass. After conducting the first part of the service, Dr Howard led his Guest Speaker to the pulpit.

Sirs, we would see Jesus.

He began his message with the words, "Sirs, we would see Jesus". I quickly forgot the man, but as he preached I was spell bound. At the end of his sermon, he bowed his head, and I like, every other person there, fell on my knees; I had seen Jesus! As he walked out, I didn't notice that he bowed to the cross. I didn't notice his dress, but I did notice his face, it shone with the love of Christ.

I didn't go into the dining hall for the evening meal but told Roy that I wasn't hungry and went and locked myself in my study, got down on my knees and asked for forgiveness, for presuming to prejudge a man who was truly God's special messenger that day. Whilst I still didn't agree with some of the things that he wrote, I loved the man.

I read his books with greater understanding, and I want to conclude by quoting from one of his books, The Christian Agnostic:

"Christianity is first and foremost a love relationship, above differences of belief; differences of worship; differences of language and colour.

Every denomination within organised religion contains a valuable truth.

The essential however is LOVING CHRIST AND LOVING ONE ANOTHER.

If a Quaker finds God in the silence, the Salvation Army in the band, the Roman Catholic in the Mass, the High Anglican through incense and ceremonial, and the Methodist through personal experience, fellowship and Charles Wesley's hymns, why talk as though this was disunity.

What matters in the end is that in our different ways we should find Christ, and love one another and have

A PASSIONATE TOGETHERNESS IN FIGHTING
ALL FORMS OF EVIL."

These are my fundamentals now.

Father and mother

Whilst we lived at Aston, and again after we moved to Alsager, we were within easy reach of my parents who lived at Mouldsworth, close to the chapel. and about one mile from the New Pale. It took us about half an hour to go over and we enjoyed going. We all went over on Christmas Day 1964 and it was good to see father at the head of the table, carving the turkey as he had always done, and looking well. Mother didn't help with the meal but just quietly watched. It was very obvious that she wasn't well. Just two weeks later I went over to Willersley Castle in Cromford, Derbyshire for a three day conference for youth workers and ministers. On the second afternoon I was attending a lecture, when one of the staff came in, and asked if Mr Challoner would come to the 'phone. It was Vera. All she said was "Eric, will you come home at once; mother is very ill."

I left immediately. It was snowing as I travelled via Buxton, and I had a very difficult journey. When I arrived home, I went straight to her bedroom and found Father, Wilfred, Herbert and Vera sitting round the bed. Vera said "Mother is asleep just now". I knelt by the bed and took her hand. My cold hand wakened her and she spoke. Her voice was very weak but I could hear what she was

Father and Mother photographed on their Golden Wedding Anniversary in 1959

saying, "Eric . . . I'm glad you came." I gave her a kiss. After a while she spoke again, "I'm very tired . . . *GOOD NIGHT. . . I WILL SEE YOU IN THE MORNING'*. She then went to sleep. Her breathing got slower and slower, and without us noticing the exact moment, it stopped. She had left us so peacefully. It was such a lovely way to go. How thankful I was that I'd arrived home in time to hear her final words. Those words took on a new significance for me. I had a God given assurance that we would 'see her in the morning'. I can't explain how or when, but I had, and still have, that strong conviction that mother was right.

Of course we were all very sad and I felt it most when I saw father weeping. I only remember him weeping once before and that was when Walter died. As a family we were so thankful that both our parents had lived so long, had been able to celebrate their Golden Wedding together and that God had blessed them in so many different ways. From a very humble beginning, when they started married life together on a small-holding at Winwick in Lancashire, they had now acquired a 'Royal Farm' - the New Pale - had four sons and a daughter, and had given us all a very good start in life. (Walter having gone ahead of mother some twenty eight years before). Father was very lost without 'his Minnie' but it was good for him that Vera and Douglas had been able to build their house in his garden and that Vera was able to 'keep an eye on him'. Without her loving care he would have had to go into a home long before he did. Mother died on 7th January 1965, aged 81, and father on 1st November (All Saints Day) 1966. We give God thanks for every precious memory of them.

CHAPTER TWELVE

THE MANSE, CHAPEL ROAD, ALDERLEY EDGE, CHESHIRE.

A church is a hospital for sinners
Not a museum for saints.

Anon.

After seven happy years in Alsager, I felt it right to move so my name was put on the list of ministers moving. I had about six enquiries, which we prayerfully considered, but the one that interested me was to the Astbury Memorial Church in Birmingham. This was a church which, in 1965, had a large and vibrant congregation, including a good number of black people. I was happy about this and went over to meet some of the people.

They couldn't have been kinder or more welcoming and they made it very clear that they wanted me to go as their minister. I wanted to go, yet deep down in my heart I hadn't got that inner conviction that it was where God wanted me to go.

I didn't get a lot of sleep that night, for I had promised to give them an answer by Friday morning. It was now Wednesday morning and I had no confirmation from the Lord, so at 6.30 am I wrote a most difficult letter to the Circuit Steward and his wife, thanking them for their kindness and generous hospitality to me, but telling them that I didn't feel able to accept. I couldn't give them any reason other than " . . . somehow I feel that God wants me to go somewhere else". Having written the letter I showed it to Sheila, who had always been so supportive in these matters, and although now disappointed she agreed that we should send it. With that, I sealed it up, put a first class stamp on it and hurried to the post. I held the letter for a moment before releasing it, but when I did, a sense of deep peace came to me and I knew that I had done the right thing.

On that same evening I was just about to go to bed when the telephone rang and a man said, "My name is Sidney Royle. I'm senior steward in the Knutsford and Alderley Edge Circuit and we were wondering if you are still free to consider an invitation to come to be our minister and live in Alderley Edge". I was speechless for a moment; *IT SO HAPPENED* that I was free and interested. I hurried to tell Sheila. We both knew that this was why we had to say no to the previous enquiries. Of course, the folk there had still to meet us and to decide if they wanted to invite us but I knew before Sidney Royle had finished his first sentence, that this was where we had to go. My one sadness was that my mother had died before hearing the news that I would be going to be a minister in the circuit where I was born and that one of the churches would be Snelson, where we all went when I was a little lad. That would have made her very happy.

The Manse, Chapel Road, Alderley Edge

And so, on September 1st 1966, we began a most interesting and exciting ministry at Alderley Edge. It's a beautiful church which looks more like an Anglican church with its tall stately spire and its clock whose chimes ring out night and day. The manse shared the church drive, so everyone who came to church came up our drive and we could see and hear all the comings and goings from our kitchen.

People who knew the area, when they heard that we were going to Alderley Edge, said "My, what a posh area, lots of wealthy business people commute to Manchester from their lovely homes there each day". Whilst that might have been true in the past, it's not the full picture today. Right from the beginning we were given a warm reception and made to feel at home. But it's always a very big ordeal for a minister, when he conducts his first service. People come to see what he looks like, to compare him with the one who has just left and to assess him.

On my first Sunday, after meeting the stewards in the minister's vestry, I was ushered into the choir vestry to have a prayer with the choir before they processed into church. It was a large choir, men and women, all wearing blue gowns. As I walked behind them into the sanctuary, I was conscious of the fact

Alderley Edge Methodist Church, Church Hall and the rear of the Manse.

that I wasn't dressed up in either cassock or gown. I never felt happy about dressing up in this way. We have no rules about it in Methodism. Some ministers do and some don't and I'm one of the latter.

I decided to put the whole matter to our Church Council, who said that they were happy for me to wear what I was most comfortable in, so I wore a gown for weddings and funerals and civic occasions, but just a clerical collar for ordinary Sunday services, (. . . I did wear a suit as well!).

The story of The Net

We had a good Sunday School and a very small Youth Club. There were about twelve of them who met in what was an old cellar. One day, two of them came to me to ask if they could have this as their own 'den' and they would be responsible for making it comfortable. I agreed and was most impressed with what they did. They cleaned it up, improved the lighting, brought a few comfortable chairs down and put pictures on the wall. The group grew and were happy.

However, one night the father of one of the girls came to collect his daughter and then came across to our house and said "Do you realise that you're breaking the law by allowing those young people to meet down there? It would be a death trap if there was a fire. It must be closed down until you have made a fire escape". So, I'm afraid that was the end of their den.

However, while they had been cleaning up in the Den, one of the lads had discovered a small square door, which he opened and discovered he could squeeze through it and climb into a space below the church hall. I was most interested in this and decided to get a torch and with a one of our youth leaders we managed to squeeze through. We were surprised to find a space of about eighteen inches beneath the large floor of the church hall.

As we came back into the den I wondered if it would be possible for us to put a girder across the full length of the den to replace the wall holding up that part of the building and then dig the soil out from beneath the church hall and so extend the den. *IT SO HAPPENED* that our organist at that time was George Yarwood, an architect, and he was very interested in the young people. I invited him to come with us down into the Den to have a look and to see if this idea was feasible.

He carefully examined the structure and all the weight that the wall was carrying and came to the conclusion that it was feasible, but that the cost of excavating all that soil and creating an underground Youth Centre, would be astronomical, and something that we as a church couldn't contemplate. Then I said "If you could satisfy the Church Trustees that it would be safe to remove the wall and replace it with a girder, we would be responsible for all the excavations and building and raising the money". He promised to do his best for us.

My brother-in-law, Douglas, is an architect, so I asked him to come over and give his opinion on the matter. He said that it could be done, but that the business of putting a girder in to carry all the weight that the wall was carrying needed great care and must only be attempted by men who were experts in these matters and who had the right equipment. This would include having about six huge hydraulic jacks which would be able carry all the weight when the wall was removed and the girder was being put in its place. The whole project could cost thousands.

IT SO HAPPENED that one of our members, Ian Marshall, was an engineer in a large firm who did this sort of thing. He came down, had a good look and was most reassuring. "With half a dozen big jacks and a couple of men I could do that all right. Leave it with me and I'll have a word with my boss. But how in the world are you going to move dozens of tons of heavy clay?" I assured him that if he could do his job, he could leave the excavating to us.

IT SO HAPPENED that the Youth Leader who had examined the space under the church hall with me was Harold Ward, a most able landscape gardener, a man of God, a man with a vision, a man with many skills, including that of dealing with young people and a man with a great love for them. He saw the possibilities that would open up if only we could get this wall safely removed.

He knew, as I knew, that young people are at their best when faced with a challenge and it would be a tremendous challenge to get them all working together in excavating the soil to create their own den. Without Harold I wouldn't have felt able to give this project my backing.

Much went on behind the scenes before we got this vision of ours accepted by the church trustees. There were many letters to be written, many meetings to be held and regulations to be met, but the fact is that they gave us the authority to go ahead. This in itself was a miracle and a real answer to our prayers.

The first job was to sink a shaft from the outside to enable us to put a ladder down and thus fulfil the fire regulations. George Yarwood had prepared detailed plans.

Ian Marshall informed us that his boss had said that if he, with two men, could take the jacks on a Saturday and return them by Monday there would be no charge and for good measure he gave us the girder. This was a most generous offer.

On the Saturday, Ian and his men arrived with the jacks and girder, but the girder couldn't be positioned in the way that Ian had planned and he came across to the Manse looking rather anxious. The only way it could be done was by cutting a hole in the wall and kitchen floor - which was above the den - and sliding it through that way. Officially, this would need a resolution from the trustees, but at one o'clock on a Saturday afternoon, with a team of experts facing a dead line, a quick decision had to be made and I made it, as Chairman of the trustees. I said to Ian "Go ahead and be it on my shoulders if there is any blame!"

Six jacks support the church

The wall was holed, the floor was opened and the huge girder was lowered into position followed by the six jacks. It was fascinating to see Ian and his mates working. The jacks were positioned and raised slowly until they could take the weight that the wall was carrying and then the top bricks of the wall were carefully removed and replaced by the girder. This was a crucial bit. The whole weight that the wall had carried was now being carried by the girder. Ian turned to me, gave the 'thumbs up' sign and said, "Eric, we're all right". I uttered a silent prayer of thanksgiving. I was very surprised how quickly they removed the wall, removed their tackle and were off by 5.30 pm. Ian and his men had done a fantastic job. I wonder how many churches have amongst their members a man not only willing but able to tackle a job like that and having for his use six huge jacks able to support the building, two men to help and, in addition, be given a girder strong enough and just the right length. *IT SO HAPPENED* that we did.

The young clay diggers

The next big job was to remove these many tons of clay. Harold Ward was not only a self-employed landscape gardener, but also a bricklayer. I asked him how much he was paid per hour for his work and suggested that we employ him at the same rate. He discovered that one of the young men who came, Derek Kenyon, was also a bricklayer and willing to help.

The clay-diggers - from an old cutting

153

Harold gradually cut down his gardening work and eventually became a full-time youth leader with us. This was the key to our success.

It was a tall order to remove a block of solid clay some seven feet deep by thirty feet long, by thirty feet across and have it taken off the premises. The clay was either dug, or pick-axed, out and a team of young people each with a shovel passed it on from one heap to the next, then at the bottom of the shaft it was put into buckets. As one empty bucket came down a full bucket was hauled up, emptied into a wheel barrow, wheeled into the car park and up a plank on to a waiting lorry, kindly loaned by Ian Webb who took it and dumped it into a pit on Chandlers farm. Lads and girls belonging to the youth club were organised into a team by Harold. It was hard work, but they enjoyed doing it and had lots of fun.

The best days of the club

Looking back, those early months when we were so busy digging, were the best days of the club. A real bond was created between us as we worked together each evening and it was a Christian atmosphere. At 9 o'clock all activity stopped and we had a ten-minute epilogue. This went on week after week, with young people working in shifts.

We did have problems of course. There was a lot of mess around the top of the shaft where all the soil was being hoisted up and in the entrance to the car park. Then as we dug below the water level, water began to seep in and very soon the young folk were working in mud. But *IT SO HAPPENED* that Roy Worth, the father of twins, was a plumber and he came down one night to see why his daughters were getting so muddy every time they came to the club. He soon found out and informed us that we bad a real problem which would get worse unless we did something about it at once. "You'll have to treat it as though you were going to build a swimming pool". He knew how to build them and told me that he would give us a helping hand with it. He supervised - in fact did - much of the work.

Although he wasn't a member and hadn't often come to our services, he now started to come regularly and eventually became one of the stewards in the church. The local bank manager, Jim Powis, came down one night and was very impressed with what he saw and he asked if he could help. He became our treasurer. The whole project involved dealing with a lot of money and he handled it all producing immaculate accounts and detailed reports.

Les. Norman, who owned the local art Gallery, took an interest in us and proved to be one of the most loyal and faithful workers. He spent night after night on duty, coming early, leaving late, always reliable. Later, when things got difficult for me and I was having to face criticism, Les was a great encourager. Although we saved thousands of pounds by all the work we were able to do with voluntary labour and through generous help, it still needed several thousands to complete the whole project and to furnish it. But we had no doubts that all our needs would be met.

Bobby Charlton opens The Net

The work began to attract publicity. A local reporter came down, was very impressed, took pictures and gave us a good write up. Soon we got on the local radio and then were featured on BBC and on ITV.

Eventually the whole project was completed, our vision had been to create a Coffee Bar, where young people could come and relax in comfortable surroundings with upholstered seating around the wall, low tables with chairs to match, soft lighting and facilities for making music.

Harold Ward revealed yet another talent; he was an artist and discovered that we had another artist in the church, Roy McLaclan. Together they designed and painted huge murals around the walls. We ran a competition amongst the young people for them to choose a name and explain why. The person who won chose

Bobby Charlton opens
The Net

Above - a coaching session with Bobby Charlton in The Net.

Right - Eric, Sheila, John and Peter in The Net.

"The Net". The reasons given were:

1 The badge of a Christian is a fish.
2 A symbol of Methodism is a shell.
3 Jesus said, "Follow me and I will make you fishers of men".

Then came the big day when we were at last ready to open. When we asked the young people whom we should invite to open it they suggested Bobby Charlton. We approached the manager of Manchester United, Mr Lou Edwards who lived in Alderley Edge, and he gave us permission to ask Bobby.

156

Bobby accepted and he and his wife came to tea with us and afterwards went to have a preview before the opening. Our John, who was then 16, was thrilled to be able to tell his mates that he had played football against Bobby Charlton and had beaten him. This was on the club's football table!

There was an impressive platform party and our church hall and The Net below were full to overflowing. I felt very proud that night and it was with a full heart that I offered this Dedication Prayer

"We thank you, O God, for all who have worked so hard to build this Coffee Bar - the Net - and we pray that it may be hallowed by your presence and that the lives of many young people will be influenced for good within these walls"

Saved from jumping to his death

Living as we did next door to the church with a youth club whose membership kept increasing was not easy. It was open five nights each week and most nights there would be some excitement - or trouble - to sort out. I remember vividly coming home from a meeting, late one night from Mobberley (the village now overshadowed by the new Manchester Airport runway) and being met by Harold Ward, who was looking very anxious. He took me round to the back of the church and there on the roof was one of our lads, John. Harold had already been up an extended ladder trying to persuade him to come down but he'd refused.

It seemed that John had come to the Net that night feeling very depressed. He was in trouble at home and he now discovered that his girl had gone off with another fellow and didn't want him any more. This was the 'last straw' and John decided that he would 'end it all' by jumping from the top of the church to his death. I climbed up and tried to persuade him to come down. He refused and managed to dislodge a piece of slate which came hurtling down the steep roof and nearly hit me. I decided to come down.

One of our key workers in the Net was Brian Mifflin, who at that time had an executive job with British Oxygen. (He later accepted God's call to the Methodist ministry). He was told about John and came to the rescue. He told John that if he would come down some of us would go and see his girl and try to persuade her to talk to him. He responded to this suggestion and came down. Brian then took him home (Brian's home) and counselled and comforted him, whilst Harold and I went off looking for the girl. By this time it was nearly midnight. We found the house but weren't able to persuade the girl to change her mind. In the meantime Brian and Pauline had calmed John down and he was soon back in the Net looking for another girl.

Trouble-maker joins the team of leaders

One of the fellows who came every night to the Net was Terry. He was a very rough diamond and had been in lots of trouble, but had great potential for good as well as for bad. He had qualities of leadership which Harold recognised and rewarded by giving him a leadership role. Instead of being a trouble-maker, his job, with Harold and myself, was to deal with trouble makers. We discovered that the young folk would take more notice of Terry for they understood his language. He became popular amongst them and was a good liaison officer between them and the other leaders and was proud of his position in the club.

Many of the young men in the Net had motor bikes. At one time I was regularly visiting them in hospital after they had been involved in accidents. One night, one of the lads had been taking his girl home from the Net when he had a tragic accident and the girl was killed. He himself escaped serious injury, but was greatly shocked and came to see Terry. Terry brought him to see me, but I was out, so Sheila took them both in and gave them coffee and comfort.

Then Terry asked if they could go into the church.

Terry takes over my job

When I arrived home I found Terry in the church, kneeling in front of the cross with his arm round his mate. I joined them. " Vic" said Terry (the young people called me 'Vic' short for Vicar) "I'm glad you've come. I'm not much good when it comes to praying, but I told God that you would be back soon and asked Him to hang on until you came". I prayed with them, then took both of them to the manse where we had a good fireside chat.

Incidentally, most ministers don't like living next door to the church, but I found that much of the vital work that we were able to do then, would probably not have been done if we had lived half a mile away.

It must have been nearly midnight when they left that night and, as they went through the door, Terry turned to me and said, "Thanks, Vic, one of these days I might be giving you a surprise". I didn't know then just what the surprise might be, but I know now and it makes me very sad as I think about it.

Terry comes to worship

Terry came from a broken home. He'd never ever been to a church service and he decided to surprise me by coming. It was most unfortunate that he chose to come on a Sunday night, when I wasn't there. Terry described to me afterwards what happened.

"I got to the church at 6.45 and heard them singing. I sat at the back and looked for you but you weren't there. There were only about twenty five folk in the church and a little fellow up in that box at the front.

I had no hymn book. I just stood up when they stood up and sat down when they sat down. The little fellow announced what was going to happen next week and then a tall chap got up, picked up a wooden plate and walked straight down the church and came to me. I assumed he wanted a sub, so I asked him how much? He just turned away and went to the rest of the people who all knew how much to give. When he'd collected all their subs, everybody stood up, so I stood up and the little fellow came down out of his box and took the money from the tall fellow, turned round, lifted it up in the air and said thank you to God for it. Then they sang another hymn and the little bloke started talking. He was dead boring. I didn't know what he was on about and I was thirsty and also dying for a fag. There was no notice to say that smoking wasn't allowed, so I lit one and sat back.

The bloke in the box stopped talking and seemed to be staring straight at me as though I had done something wrong. The tall fellow who collected the subs turned round, got up and came straight down the church, opened the door and told me to leave. I didn't know what I'd done wrong and he didn't explain. I'll not be going again, Vic".

Terry was both angry and hurt. I could have wept. I was sad that so little love and understanding had been shown to one who didn't know he had done wrong, when he came to worship for the very first time.

A dream come true

The night that Bobbie Charlton declared the net 'Open' was a dream come true as far as I was concerned. We spared no expense in the furnishing, fitting coffee and tea making facilities - and a well-equipped shop. There were games to play; chess, draughts and other board games, a very popular football game and a dart-board. It was open five nights each week with a rota of volunteer helpers on duty each night.

Our numbers grew until we had an average attendance each night of over one hundred and on Fridays at the Disco even more. They loved to come. Some came five nights a week and would be waiting at the door for us to open. It was 'home from home' for them. The Net was part of the work of the church, but we never said, "If you come to the Net you must come to church". We were criticised for this, but I felt that the Net was the Church and at 9 o'clock each night everything stopped, the bar closed and all assembled in the hall for a ten minute epilogue, followed by notices and announcements. The Sunday Night at Eight was their Sunday service and we did try to find speakers to challenge and inspire. But the whole ethos of the club was Christian, run by Christians and based on Christian principles and for two years all went well.

A dream that was becoming a nightmare

I wish that the story could have continued on such an optimistic note, but alas this was not to be. Any one who has had any experience of dealing with a club of this nature, especially with the numbers that we had, knows that problems will arise . . . and they did!

Friday night was the night when the choir met to practice. It was also the club disco night. The two were in adjoining rooms. The young people always wanted loud music and kept the volume turned up. Imagine the choir practising "Sheep may safely graze" and a crowd of young people in the next room jiving.

I remember an irate choir master coming to the manse on one occasion and asking me to come and face the choir and to listen to what they had to put up with. I went. It was an impossible situation. They said "Friday night has always been choir practice night, so why should we have to move?" I agreed with them, so we decided to have the disco on Saturday night.

It wasn't only the choir that were upset. Chapel Road, Alderley Edge was a very 'superior' residential road. The houses were heavily rated and some of the residents got together and demanded that the Club be closed or their rates reduced. One Sunday afternoon, two residents came to our front porch and emptied a big bag of litter that they had collected in the road - chip papers, packets, bottles and tins - with a note saying "Your youngsters forgot to take these home last night." Sheila and I were both very upset.

We have always been happy with our neighbours and we did sympathise with them and were most embarrassed by this.

The vast majority of the young people were fine, but when a few came from the pub having been drinking, this meant trouble. Drink wasn't allowed on the premises and when those on the door prevented them from going in, they made trouble in the road. We called the police, but they could do very little. It only needs a handful of youngsters who are determined to wreck a club of this nature to do so.

I was heartbroken. I felt sorry for Harold Ward our Leader. No one could have done more than he did and he was supported by a very loyal group of voluntary workers.

I had promised to stay seven years and when the time came for me to leave it was decided that the Net should close. I'm sure of this, that for several years the Net brought much happiness and great blessing to many young people, but the conflict of interests between the Club and the Church and the destructive power of a few wreckers was too much for us.

Pastor Harold Ward!

Harold Ward who, throughout it all, had been supported by his wife Pam, enrolled as a student at Alsager Teacher Training College, (now part of the Manchester Metropolitan University) and then went on to Keele University to get his degree. Later he felt called to a full-time ministry in the church and went for further training to the Northern Theological College at Didsbury, then was accepted and ordained in the United Reformed Church. He asked to be given a 'tough assignment'. This was typical of Harold. They sent him to Wythenshawe, Manchester, to a church on one of the largest housing estates in the country and which was 'run down' and ready to close.

There was much poverty and deprivation, but he managed to establish a base from which he was able to meet the needs of many people. Those with no

Harold Ward (left) with Eric and Peter, 1983

previous church background came to his services. He married couples who couldn't afford a 'posh wedding'. Not only did the church not charge them, but provided the bride with her wedding dress and clothes for bridesmaids. He also set up a collecting centre for clothes and furniture etc. which he freely distributed to needy families and helped in many other practical ways.

He has many interesting stories to tell. One in particular amused me. When he had a baptism, the church would lay on a meal for the family. On one occasion the baby's father came to see Harold to arrange the date of the baptism and said that they would have to wait until uncle Norman came out of gaol, for he was going to be a godfather.

They did wait and uncle Norman came and made a fuss of the baby and was most friendly towards Harold and grateful for what he was doing. "If I can help you, Pastor, in any way, let me know. He looked round, saw that they had no candles in the church, so he said, "Pastor, I know where there are two that would just suit this place. I'm sure they would never miss them!" Harold thanked him, but declined the offer. I hope that Harold himself will one day write his story.

He came to see me recently and read my account of the opening of the Net and of the 'Dream that became a Nightmare'. His comment was that the seeds that were sown in the hearts of those young people were bearing fruit today. I was most encouraged to hear that young couples who had met in the Net and later married, were sending their children to church and that Terry, who was thrown out of church, now was happily married. He also had a good report about John who threatened to jump off the church roof.

161

He told of a couple much loved by the other members and who had married. The girl was disabled and her husband tragically died in his early forties. Harold was asked to take his funeral. About one hundred came, most of whom knew Harold and remembered the Net with affection. The very latest news that I heard is that some young people, children of Net members, are hoping to restore it and perhaps open it again, but on a much smaller scale.

A little church with a big problem

One morning two ladies from one of my smaller churches came to see me. They said that the church had a big problem. I hadn't been aware of any problem. They asked "Haven't you noticed that all the congregation sit at one side of the church except 'old Tom'?" (that wasn't his real name). I confessed that I had noticed it, but didn't know why. She then said "The reason is Tom smells and no one wants to sit near to him. A week next Sunday is our Harvest Festival, the church will be full and we feel that someone ought to do something about it before then. We've approached Social Services and they arranged for a male nurse to give him a bath, but Tom refused to let him in".

I did know Tom and asked them to leave the matter with me. He had lived alone for several years, ever since his wife died and did neglect himself. However I didn't think that he would be very happy if I told him that the folk at the chapel were complaining that he smelled.

It was a difficult situation. As I thought about it prayerfully I decided I would go and see Frank Reid. Frank was a postman. He knew Tom and got on well with him. I explained the problem and we decided that I would take him to Frank's for tea, and during the visit Frank would cut his hair. The biggest problem would be getting him undressed and in the bath.

It was arranged for the Saturday afternoon just before the Harvest Festival. When I called, Tom had forgotten all about it, but was happy to get in the car. He never bothered locking his door so I went back into the house and quickly collected all the clothes that he needed and put them in a black plastic bag. When we arrived at Frank's he gave us a cup of tea. He then reminded Tom that it was the Harvest Festival the next day and that it would be a good idea for him to have a hair cut. He agreed to this and all seemed to be going well so far. It was a struggle to get him up the stairs but we managed with me pulling and Frank pushing and when in the bathroom sat him on a chair. Frank put a tea towel round his neck and started cutting his hair, while I ran the water in the bath and began to remove his boots. Having removed his boots I then began to pull off his very dirty socks. This wasn't easy, but after a struggle I managed it. Tom didn't like this. He hadn't had those socks off for a long time and his feet were sore. It was no wonder, for his toe-nails hadn't been cut for ages and had begun to coil round. Neither Frank nor I had ever seen anything like this. It must have made it very difficult for him to walk.

All this time Frank was snipping away at his hair. Then he told him that we were going to give him a lovely warm bath. I don't think he heard or didn't take it in, for he made no protest. Frank began to undo his shirt buttons and I his trouser buttons. He didn't say much, but he held on to the buttons. Poor old Tom. We weren't rough with him, but firm and just as we had a shock when we took his socks off, we had another shock when we took his shirt off - he had another underneath - and after taking his vest off, he had another vest underneath and the last one looked as though it had been on a long time. No wonder Tom smelled.

Having managed to remove all his clothes, I caught hold of his feet and Frank lifted under his arm pits and we gently lowered him into the bath. I made sure that the water wasn't too hot and once he was in he lay back and really enjoyed it. We let him soak for some time and then began to give him a good wash from head to toe, including a shampoo and a shave.

I took all his clean clothes out of the black plastic bag and replaced them with his dirty ones, tied it up and put it in the dust bin. We then put his vest, pants and shirt on. I had the job of dealing with his toe-nails. It hurt him, but Frank had some good clippers for the job and I used them carefully. We then put on his socks and trousers, followed by his jacket. He looked a new man and really smart and as he sat at the table for tea, there was no doubt that Tom was a happy man and the smile on his face showed it.

The next day I took the Harvest Festival. The place was full, the members had made an impressive display of flowers and vegetables, but my eyes were on Tom, who sat there, looking very smart, with a smile on his face. He was surrounded by people, including the two ladies who came to see me about their 'problem', and they too had a smile on their faces and sang with extra gusto our opening hymn 'Come, ye thankful people, come'.

God's special people

In addition to having pastoral charge of four churches, I was also a visiting chaplain at two centres: the David Lewis Centre where they had over two hundred men, women and children who suffered from severe epilepsy, and the Mary Dendy Homes - an Institution for people who had various psychiatric disorders and included about one hundred and twenty who suffered from Down's Syndrome.

Each Sunday morning at 9.30 I held a special service for the Down's Syndrome people and this was always followed by morning service in one of my churches. This meant a big rush for me.

I enjoyed these services at Mary Dendy and loved the people. They were very affectionate and wanted to both give and receive affection. After the service they all wanted to shake hands with me and this began to take almost as long as the service. I discussed the problem with matron and we decided that at the end of

163

each service they would form a large circle round the hall and stretch their right hand out and I would hurry past and try to touch each outstretched hand. It was good fun.

I prepared carefully a Bible-based story each Sunday, always stressing the fact that they were each VERY SPECIAL and that God loved them. They hung on every word. To help them remember this, instead of a benediction, I got them to hold their left hand up and stretch out their fingers.

Then, grasping their little finger they would say after me, "GOD"; holding their next finger they would say "LOVES"; then their tallest finger and holding it tight they would shout, "ME". I remembered the words of Jesus, "Except you become as little children you cannot enter the Kingdom of Heaven." These folk had a childlike faith, (not childish), and a depth of spirituality that I've seldom found anywhere. I counted it a great privilege to be their minister.

CHAPTER THIRTEEN

25 LEEK ROAD, CHEADLE

And now these three remain;
Faith, hope and love,
But the greatest of these is love.
1 Corinthians 13:13 (NIV)

After we had been at Alderley Edge for seven years I was invited to become the superintendent minister of the Cheadle (Staffs) circuit. As always we were sad to leave old friends and also such a lovely area.  However, we very soon felt at home among new friends and discovered, to our delight that, almost on our doorstep, we had the Churnet valley and the Manifold valley. Also one of my churches was actually within the Peak District and another one in the village of Alton near the famous Towers. We had a pleasant four-bedroomed manse with a very long back garden which had got so overgrown a cow could have hidden in it at the far end. Pongo was in his element. I enjoyed tackling this and was able to borrow a tractor and rotovator and transformed it into a good vegetable and fruit garden.

An American invasion causes confusion

This appointment included the chaplaincy of a women's prison and I thought that this would be a new and interesting challenge. It also meant that I was back again in the Chester and Stoke District - my home District. My prison chaplaincy experiences are in a separate chapter. Here, I want to begin by telling of a mission that in the beginning went disastrously wrong and in the end miraculously right.

It all began with a 'phone call from Maurice Barnett, the minister at Westminster Central Hall, London.

Maurice asked me if my circuit would like to have an American Lay Witness Mission, conducted by a team of fifteen, part of a much larger group who would be missioning in different parts of the country. They would come on a Thursday afternoon and leave on a Monday morning. He gave such a glowing report of previous missions that I was persuaded to accept them. After having arranged hospitality for fifteen for four nights, I had a 'phone call from America on Monday midnight to say they would be coming on Friday, not Thursday. On Friday afternoon the courier of the coach 'phoned from Chester asking for directions to the church and saying that they would be arriving about 5.30 pm with our party of five! So I had the unenviable task of letting ten of the hosts know that they wouldn't be having their guests. At that time I hadn't been well. I'd seen a heart specialist, who diagnosed angina and I was having medication which tended to slow me down. If I had too much stress then I was in trouble. When the coach arrived I felt like telling them to stay on it! However, none of the five had any idea that we had been caused any inconvenience. When they did hear they were most distressed. Our people who had been so badly let down were upset, but when the five went into the church hall, they still gave them a welcome.

A lay witness mission American style

However, in spite of this, the first rally on the Friday night went well. On Saturday morning we had arranged informal meetings in different homes – 'Coffee Groups'. After coffee and brief introductions there followed a sharing time. The atmosphere was very relaxed and people who had never spoken about their own personal faith before felt able to do so. What was it about these people that enabled them to make such an impact in such a short time on so many people, after such a disastrous start?

Where there is great love miracles can happen

On the front of the pulpit before they spoke they hung a poster with these words on it: "Where there is great love miracles can happen", and miracles did happen in the lives of a number of people and whole families. On the Sunday they shared in different services around the circuit. They didn't preach; they simply witnessed to the difference it made in their lives when they discovered for themselves that they were each very special to God and that He loved them, had a purpose for them and their eternal destiny was safe in His keeping. A United Rally was held at Cheadle at eight o'clock on Sunday night. My colleague Ralph Dale still says that it was the most powerful meeting that he had ever been in. Our own people were witnessing to the fact that God had become real to them.

Lives had been changed

From the beginning, some had opposed the whole idea of the Lay Witness weekend saying it would be 'just a flash in the pan' and that when the Americans left so would their influence. Now, over twenty years later, I could take you into many homes of people who would still say that it was the most memorable weekend of their lives.

The minister is healed

Amongst those who could count their blessings, was the minister. I had three reasons never to forget that weekend.

1 The utter frustration before they came.

2 My healing, as a result of their coming.

3 The miracle that followed their coming.

The first I have described.

Regarding the others; I have mentioned that the medication that I was having for angina tended to slow me down, and because of all the extra things that I had to do at that time I very foolishly decided to stop taking the pills just for the weekend. During the service on the Sunday night I sat in front of the pulpit facing the congregation completely absorbed in what was going on. Their leader, Ed, was in charge and when he closed the service he turned to me and in a tone of authority said "Will you go into your vestry and sit down". He and two of the others followed me in. He looked at me and said, "Eric, you are a very sick man, but God is going to heal you". (It seemed that my face was white and my lips blue). He placed one hand on my head and asked the other two to do the same. Then he said a very simple prayer asking God in Christ's name to heal me. He told me not to stop taking my pills without consulting my doctor. We then went out to speak to the congregation as they left. I went home, feeling a bit dazed, but didn't have any pain. I didn't sleep much that night but for another reason which I will explain later. I went to see my doctor and told him how much better I felt and asked if I could now stop taking my pills. He was a bit reluctant to say yes, but suggested I could try it for a time to see how I went on. I have never taken another pill for angina since that day, neither have I had any sign of the illness since!

The recipe for a miracle

I suppose that it's true to say that my healing could be classed as a miracle, but I want now to tell you of another. It was during that final service when Ed was preaching, that he leaned forward and looked round the congregation and said slowly "Does any one here want to see a miracle happen in this Church which will bring blessing?" I certainly did, and listened intently as he went on to say, "Now think of one person in this church that you don't like." He then paused, giving us each plenty of time to think. I didn't need any time for one name came up at once, it was George. He was a most gifted local preacher and held important offices both in the church and in the District. He was older and in some things much more able than I was; he knew it and I knew it too. He had made life difficult for me at times and I'm sorry to say that we didn't like each other. So, what next ? Ed went on, "You must go to that person and TELL THEM THAT YOU LOVE THEM!" Well, I knew that I couldn't do that. In the first place it would be a lie and what a fool I would feel, and I knew that he wouldn't believe me. No, this must be for someone else, but not me.

"George I love you"

Ed left us with this challenge, announced the closing hymn and after that I was ushered into the vestry and received the laying on of hands and prayer for healing. This for the time being made me forget the challenge, but that night I couldn't sleep for I knew in my heart that it was a word for me, even though it didn't make sense. The question was, was I willing to be a fool for Christ? At breakfast I shared my burden with Sheila. Her reply was, "If you really feel like that you must go and I'll pray for you". I felt like replying "No, you go and I'll pray for you."

I finished breakfast, got on my bicycle and hurried to George's home about half a mile away. I think that it was one of the hardest things that I've had to do. When I got there I rang the bell and his wife came to the door. Now that evening it was the Annual General Meeting of the Church Property Committee when important appointments were to be made. George was senior Property Steward, an office that he had held for years, and he would be up for re-election at the meeting. She knew this, but what she didn't know was that the other two Property Stewards had threatened to resign if he was reappointed. She was probably expecting trouble, but she greeted me kindly and invited me in to the front room where George sat reading. He didn't get up, but asked me to sit down, which I did, in an armchair facing him - and quite close. Looking straight at him, I simply said, "GEORGE, I'VE COME TO TELL YOU THAT I LOVE YOU". He never said a word, just stared in blank amazement, feeling sure that I must have 'flipped my lid'. There was an awkward silence, which I broke by saying, "I know that I haven't always acted as though I did and I'm sorry." Then he said "Well, I suppose that I haven't always acted as though I did either."

A new man brings a new spirit to the meeting

What followed was something quite remarkable. For the first time in all the years that we had known each other, we were able to be open and frank, each acknowledging our mistakes, our differences and each being sorry. This conversation must have gone on for almost twenty minutes and ended with him saying "Shall we pray together?" We knelt by our armchairs and he prayed. When we got up on our feet we shook hands and I can honestly say that I felt a real love for him. This surely was a miracle. At the meeting that evening we quickly sailed through the preliminaries and when we came to the appointments George asked if he could speak. There was dead silence. He stood up - which was unusual - and then told us just how long he had held this office in the church and how much he had enjoyed it; but perhaps the time had come for someone else to take over his job and if so he would be happy for them to do so. This was a new George who was speaking, but only two of us knew what had happened; George and I. Then one of those who was going to resign if we re-appointed him spoke. "Well, George, you've done a good job over the years and although we haven't always agreed with you, hearing you talk like this, I'm happy to propose that we re-elect you." The other trustee seconded the proposal and it was carried unanimously. There came a new spirit into the church and although we still didn't see eye to eye over some things George and I became friends. When I left Cheadle he was in hospital and the very last person that I went to see before retiring was dear George. Now I could say and mean it,

"GEORGE, I LOVE YOU."

He is in heaven now.

God's mountaineer

In July 1980, I was a representative at the Methodist Conference in Sheffield. One rather hot afternoon, I decided to leave the conference hall and go to the refreshment room for a cup of tea. There weren't many people in there at the time, but I noticed an old fellow who looked as though he had wandered in from the street hoping to get a cup of tea. I decided to go and sit by him and have a chat. Little did I realise just what would be the outcome of that decision. As I sat down I said "Do you mind if I come and sit by you?" He stretched out his hand and said "Please do, my name is Bert and I come from Dudley." I replied "My name is Eric and I come from Cheadle in Staffordshire." Then began a most interesting and thrilling conversation, with Bert doing all the talking. He told me that his father had been a Methodist minister and that he had been a Probation Officer before his retirement and that his main interest in life was his Bible Class, in the Vicar Street Methodist Church in Dudley. He said that he began the class in 1925 and fifty five years later it was still going strong and that during this period over twenty members of the class had become ministers. He told how, in one of his studies, the subject was 'mountains' and they decided that they would have a holiday together climbing the highest mountain in Britain, Ben Nevis. On the top of the mountain they found such a wonderful peace and at the bottom in the town of Fort William they found a group of Christians with whom they became very friendly and who like them had climbed Ben Nevis and found a peace there.

Bert's Peace Cairn on the mountain

IT SO HAPPENED that on August 15th, 1945, the Dudley group were on holiday again in Fort William when they heard the-news that the war had ended. They met their Fort William friends and decided to celebrate this good news by building a Peace Cairn on the top of Ben Nevis. Having built it they thought it would be good for others to share in this project. So Bert started writing to different people and groups. He told me that it has now become an International Peace Cairn, having in it a stone from Everest sent by Sir Roger Hunt; a tablet from the Scouts of America and another representing the Youth of the United Nations. The one that he was most proud of was the tablet sent by the Mayor of

Hiroshima, Mr Setsua Yamada, "A wonderful ambassador of peace" said Bert enthusiastically. The mayor sent it carefully packed in a wooden crate and it was consecrated in the Vicar Street Methodist church. From there it was transported to Fort William and with the help of the Mountain rescue team taken to the top and built into the Cairn. *IT SO HAPPENED* that when the tablet was taken from the church in Dudley, two pieces of the wooden crate were accidentally left behind and the group decided to have them made into a cross and to call it 'The Hiroshima Cross'. Then Bert took it to Coventry Cathedral, where it was placed in their Chapel of Unity.

I was thrilled just to listen to Bert and in a very short time felt that I had known him all my life. It was time to go back into the Conference hall and as I left him he said "Brother Eric, if you would ever like to use this cross at any time I could arrange for you to borrow it". I jumped at this offer as *IT SO HAPPENED* that I had been booked to speak at an ecumenical service on Remembrance Sunday that year. So in November, Bert went to Coventry Cathedral, collected his precious cross and came by train to Crewe where I met him and brought him to our home. What a delightful guest he was.

An ambassador for peace

Sitting in our lounge he continued his fascinating story. He told how the Dudley and Fort William Groups had sent two tablets inscribed with messages of peace to Japan, to be put in the Hiroshima Peace garden and how he had been invited to go to Japan, as guest of the Japanese government. There he visited Hiroshima and met some of the survivors who were still suffering. There were tears in his eyes as he recalled some of the things that he heard and saw. He went on to say, "Yet, from this very city, came a message of peace and reconciliation and good will." I'm glad that I was able to record on tape Bert's conversation with me. I have listened again to his voice and include now his closing words:

Left - Bert Bissell. Right - The Hiroshima Cross

"Whenever I climb to our Peace Cairn, I think of the millions of youth who were slaughtered in two world wars and imagine them saying to me 'Surely there's a better way to settle disputes than by destroying the lives of some of the most promising young people in the world. Try to settle things by peaceful means.'" Bert continued; "I feel that this is one of the jobs that our class has been called to do and I feel that God has given us the Hiroshima Cross to help us to do it. So whoever hears this tape, I do pray that you will decide to dedicate your life to Christian service of love, reconciliation and peace."

In 1987 Bert Bissell, at the age of 85, became the joint winner of the World Methodist Peace Award. A truly remarkable man. I felt privileged to take the Hiroshima cross to the Remembrance Day service and to be able to tell some of Bert's inspiring story.

I'm so thankful that I went to speak to him that day in July and for the way that our conversation opened a door to a real mountain top experience for me.

Mercy mission to earthquake victims

On New Year's Day 1981 an urgent appeal was made on behalf of the Methodist Relief Fund, for 100 caravans for the homeless earthquake victims in Southern Italy. This prompted local farmer, Alfred Leese, who was our Circuit Steward, to come and see me with the suggestion that our circuit be responsible for providing one. We offered our van, but Alfred had heard of a bigger one for sale for £400. The money had to be raised very quickly and through the generosity of our people this four-berth 16.5 cwt caravan was soon paid for, together with enough money to insure it, pay for the ferry crossing and the petrol to tow it to Italy.

Alfred, along with his brother Edward from Lichfield, volunteered to take the

caravan to Southern Italy, despite the fact that neither had ever driven on the Continent before. They used Alfred's car and equipped it with snow chains in case they were needed. I'll never forget that snowy Sunday in January, when at 12 noon after the morning service the caravan was dedicated, and Alfred and Edward set off on their hazardous journey into the unknown. A very moving moment. They drove day and night and arrived back in record time, exhausted, but happy that they had been able to provide a home for an Italian family.

CHAPTER FOURTEEN

I WAS IN PRISON

He breaks the power of cancelled sin
He sets the prisoner free.
Charles Wesley

When I tell people that I was in prison their first reaction is surprise. Prison is for bad people - so they think - and I assume that they didn't include me in that group. I hasten to tell them that I was in prison as a chaplain - appointed by the Home Office of her Majesty's Government - with a special concern for Methodist prisoners and all others who were not registered either as Anglicans or Roman Catholics (they had their own chaplain). I was part-time, having also the responsibility of the superintendent minister of the Cheadle circuit. It was a women's prison called Moor Court (quite close to Alton Towers) having about 120 inmates.

Although it was called an 'open prison', which meant that it wasn't surrounded by high walls and locked doors, there was a ring of security around it and a careful check was made five times each day. The main prison building had once been a manor house with a large garden, to which were added workshops and farm buildings. In the day time prisoners wore clothes suitable for the job that they were doing and after they had finished their work they changed into their own clothes. Some worked in the gardens, others on the farm, feeding pigs, calves, poultry etc. and cleaning out their sheds, Others were in the workshops doing a variety of tedious jobs like putting electric plugs together, making the clothes for small dolls and soldiers, all time consuming and repetitive. A number worked in the kitchen and others were cleaners. They finished work at 4.30 pm, had a drink, got washed and changed, wrote letters, watched TV or relaxed in the games room.

The prisoners were there for a great variety of reasons. Some served the whole of their sentence at Moor Court, usually nine months or less. Others faced a much longer sentence and had served the first part in a closed prison such as Holloway or Styal, coming to Moor Court for the final stint. These included the 'lifers', which meant that they had been given a 'life sentence'. In practice this meant, serving about ten years, if they behaved themselves for that time. These would come to Moor Court for the final six or nine months of their sentence. I was surprised to discover that many of these preferred the closed prison because it was such a terrible temptation to run away from an open one. When first appointed I went to see the Governor, a very imposing lady. She gave me a warm welcome and then said "I'm afraid, Mr Challoner, we don't get many Methodists here." I told her that I was glad about that and that it wasn't our policy in the church to recruit clients for her establishment! I went each Thursday and spent the whole afternoon and evening there. My first duty was to report to the governor or deputy governor to see if any new prisoners for whom I was pastorally responsible had arrived since my previous visit. Whilst their records were available for me to see, I generally chose not to. If they wanted to tell me their story, I would listen.

Whose side are you on?

A prison chaplain has to be very careful. He has a pastoral concern for both staff and prisoners, but first and foremost his job is to care for the prisoners. Many of them despised some members of the staff and for the chaplain to fraternise with these could damage his relationship with the prisoners. I had carefully and prayerfully to win their trust and respect. This wasn't easy, but once I had done this I enjoyed my visits and found them very rewarding. I had pastoral responsibility for Methodists and 'other denominations' which included Jews, Muslims, Gypsies and those without any 'religious labels'. In practice any who came seeking help, or wished to attend my services were never turned away. I visited them as they worked on the farm, in the garden and in the workshops, I had my evening meal with them, sitting wherever there was a vacant place. The tables were for four. After the meal we had a service in the chapel, which had been tastefully furnished and included an organ, a raised low platform and reading desk, We usually found a prisoner who could play. If not, I would get an organist to come from Cheadle,

Prisoners were free to attend. The numbers varied, but often we had twenty or thirty. After each service I held a clinic which was for any with a special need or concern they wanted to share with me. Often it was a concern about the well being of a child or husband or close relative and my pastoral care included these, but I did have to consult the Governor before making contact with those outside the prison. Some of the saddest situations occurred when the husband didn't want his wife back, or parents their daughter, There was a wide variety of prisoners including shoplifters; women who were inadequate house keepers, perhaps with a young family and either no husband, or one who was out of work, and who found the big stores too much of a temptation. "It's not easy, padre, when you have two hungry little lads at home and no money to buy them anything", as one young mother once said to me. There were also professional shoplifters, who became rich on their 'takings' and who loved to boast about how they did it.

The Duchess

We always seemed to have a number of prostitutes from Birmingham and London. I question why they were penalised and the men involved weren't. These were in some ways not unlike the shoplifters; two groups, one trying to support a family by their earnings and the other group who were professionals working under the control of a pimp. They seemed to make plenty of money. During the nine years that I was at Moor Court the one person that I found the most despicable and offensive was a pimp. She dressed in expensive clothes and was called the 'Duchess', Prisoners were afraid of her and officers seem to ignore her. In the television room there was a long settee. This was her 'throne'. She didn't sit on it, but lay across it, leaving room for no one else. She always seemed to have plenty of cigarettes to smoke, which she did using a very long holder. She despised the prison officers and she despised me and made it very obvious. I felt that woman was really wicked and was glad when she left,

"I killed my mother"

One day I had a 'phone call from the prison, asking if I would come in - the governor wanted to see me. I was told that a prisoner who had just arrived and who was 'one of mine', had attempted suicide and was in great need of pastoral care. She was a girl of twenty-four and she came from a good home, and had never been in trouble with the police before. She had had a very responsible job and was accused of fraud. When she went to court, her parents accompanied her. She was found guilty and sentenced to nine months in prison. Upon hearing the sentence, her mother had a heart attack and died in the court. The whole family turned against her. She hated herself and didn't want to live. All she could say was, "I killed my mother, I killed my mother." The Governor gave me a free hand to do what I could. I got in touch with her father, who at first didn't want to talk to me. Much prayer went up for that family. It was an impossible situation, but I'm glad to say that prayers were answered. Her father came to see her, realised how desperately she had suffered and forgave her, but she found it very difficult to forgive herself. That was a very dark patch in my chaplaincy work.

Case of mistaken identity

One of the finest Christians that I've ever met was at Moor Court. Her name was Myrtle, she was black and she came from Handsworth, Birmingham. Lots of prisoners would protest about being wrongfully convicted but not Myrtle, although I believe that she had been. She said to me "Pastor, the Lord had a job for me to do here", and I agreed. This is what happened. Myrtle was the leader of the Women's Meeting in her Pentecostal Church. It was Saturday, her husband was at work and she had got lunch ready for her three children - boys of seventeen and fourteen and a girl of twelve. She sent the elder boy to fetch his brother in. He saw him running quickly towards home when a police car stopped and an officer got out and started to put him into the police car. The elder boy ran to them and tried to restrain the officer and to find out what was wrong. By this time Myrtle herself came out and saw two policemen trying to put the eldest boy in the car. She ran to them and vigorously intervened. A crowd, mainly of black youths, quickly gathered and some began throwing stones and a very angry situation developed. More police cars arrived, then the crowd dispersed and Myrtle and her two sons were arrested and taken off to the police station and she was eventually given a three months sentence for ' assaulting a police officer'. The two boys were released and it was later discovered that the younger one was quite innocent - it was a case of 'mistaken identity'.

When I spoke to Myrtle's pastor, he confirmed this story and said that the whole community had been shocked. The family was well known and well respected. She was such an inspiration in the prison. Never once did she complain - but always had a smile and often would sing some gospel songs. Her presence transformed our services in the chapel, At that time one of my members from Cheadle, Barbara Thorley, accompanied me and played the organ. She and Myrtle became good friends. When she left we were all sorry to see her go, but so glad for her sake, When she got home she wrote the following letter.

Myrtle's letter

"Dear Pastor, Good day and my best regards to you and your family. . .

your lovely card I have received and was most grateful for your concern and thoughtfulness. I also will express my thanks to you and Barbara for the lovely moments you all shared with me during my sentence. May the Lord give to you and her strength and good health for your caring work. I'm OK and still holding on strong to my Lord. My release from prison was a blessed one. Wednesday night I was able to attend our Fellowship, on Friday I went to our church service and Communion and on Saturday we had a lovely concert and on Sunday a baptism which was lovely. I enjoyed every moment Well pastor, I'm so thankful to God . . . who through trials and tribulations . . . kept me and my family. Please remember me to your church and thank them for their prayers."

Well, we didn't get another Myrtle, but the idea that all prisoners are bad is wrong. We all have need to say, "There but for the grace of God go I."

When mum is in prison

When a mother is sent to prison it's often the whole family which is sentenced too, especially the children. I wrote many letters to try to comfort and reassure them that their mother was all right and often had letters in reply. Here are extracts from just two:

"Dear sir, Thank you for your very nice letter. I'm so pleased you went to see my mum and had supper with her, It helps her to be able to talk to someone. I have been learning First Aid for sixteen weeks at a sicreatic

(her spelling) *hospital and we also had to learn the discomfort of sitting on a bedpan, . ."*

(I tried to picture them doing that),

" *. . and being bandaged the wrong way. I hope one day to become a midwife. I think that it's a miracle that anyone is ever born. Thank you for going to see my mum, it was very kind Yours sincerely, Helen PS Could you please pray for me, nana, granddad and mum. Oh and a little prayer for my doggy who has an ulcer on his paw."*

My last letter is a real treasure, so beautifully written and she took trouble to decorate it with stars. Sally was put into a home for children in need of care alongside many who were there because they had done wrong. This hurt her mum very much and Sally resented it too.

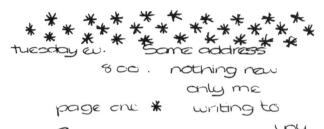

tuesday ev.   Same address
              8 oo .   nothing new
                      only me
      page one *   writing to
                             you.

Dear Rev. Challoner,
                    It was really
nice hearing from you and it
comforts me to know that
you are looking after my mum.
It is really nice of you to
remember me in your prayers.
I dont know if my mum knows
but I am so unhappy here. I
guess when my mum comes
home and we will be together
and then I'd be happy.

* page two   *

I'm sure you understand my
feelings and how unhappy I
am. (But please dont tell my mum
because she won't be able to
carry on with her sentence) The
little card you sent me was
so beutifull and kind so thank
you very much (I will cherish it
always.) here is a little poem.

   I dont know you all that
   well
   although I dont i know I can
   tell
   that you are troughtful and
   kind aswell.
I hope you liked that. I made it

*   Page three . *

up all by myself. Well at the moment I am watching a film called
Maggie. It is so boring. Oh yes!!
Its not worth sealing your letters
with selotape because they
just get opened and its wasting
your selotape. Well I havent
much to write so until I write
again love and best wishes
    Sally·xxx
P.S. Please write soon because
your letters cheer me up.
And I'll remember you in my
prayes as well xx

Mary Bell

I mentioned before that prisoners who had been used to being in a closed prison often preferred that to Moor Court. One such was Mary Bell. At one time her name was headline news as being the girl who, at the age of ten, had been found guilty of the manslaughter of a little lad of three and another of four. She was described as a 'monster' and was given a life sentence. When she came to Moor Court from Styal in June 1977 she had already been nine years in prison and was now a young woman of twenty. She was a Roman Catholic, so I wasn't informed of her arrival. I was having my tea there one Thursday, sitting at a table with three young women and was very impressed with one of them who was a newcomer. She was different. She seemed intelligent and told me that she was working on the farm and was quite enthusiastic about a new litter of pigs they had. Her hobby was drawing and I saw a book that she carried around, with many drawings in it, which revealed she was a skilled artist. It was a great shock and surprise to me when I was told that this was Mary Bell, the girl who had been described as a monster. I couldn't imagine any one less like a monster. She was quietly spoken, tastefully dressed and seemed always to be busy either reading or drawing.

When she came to Moor Court she was so excited, for it meant she was on her last stint and would soon be able to apply for her parole, the one thing that she lived for. Her expectations were heightened when she was asked if she would like to go on a typing course; this was to help her get a job when she was free. Then came a shattering blow. For reasons that were never given to Mary, the Parole Board had refused her application. This was the second time this had happened. On the previous occasion she wrote to her mother and the poem she sent to her was quoted in the News of the World on 18th September 1977. Here is an extract:

THE PAIN, THE LONELY DAYS

No one will ever know
The pain, the lonely days.
Never understand the sorrow of being caged away.
They'll never see a sunset through ugly black steel bars,
Or see the moon as I do, or stories in the stars.
They won't know of my awful misery
The existing from day to day,
Just dying every second
Wasting my life away.
Yet I don't feel bitter toward anyone,
I just have to bear my cross
Like everyone else in this world
Gaining with every loss.

And now for the second time, her hopes were dashed. I heard about it from one of the other prisoners when I arrived on the Thursday following the verdict, and as soon as I saw Mary I could see she had been devastated by the verdict. Several women asked me to have a word with her, so I told them to get her to come to see me in the Chapel after the service. When Mary came in with a friend, I was already talking to someone. She waited for a short time and then ran out, I never saw her again, but I was very conscious that something was seriously wrong and that the prisoners knew things that I didn't know.

A 'monster' on the run???

The next day my worst fears were confirmed. Radio Stoke broadcast that Mary Bell, together with another prisoner - a convicted prostitute - had escaped from Moor Court. It was later in the National news and in all the papers. The picture that the world was given was of an escaped monster. Mothers kept a special eye on their children and the police throughout the country were on the alert to recapture 'this dangerous criminal'. As I heard and read, I could have wept. This girl, in my opinion wasn't a dangerous criminal. What she had done was a very terrible thing, and if it had have been our two little lads that she had killed, my attitude to her might have been totally different. I can well imagine the anger and bitterness that people feel in such cases. I was very limited in my contacts but the impression I got was that she wasn't aware of the enormity of her crime. She was only ten years old when she did this dreadful thing. If I had have been consulted, I would have recommended her for parole. People who have to make these decisions have a very difficult job, especially when there has been a blaze of publicity and I don't envy them, but pray for them.

The other prisoner, who was much older and knew her way around, took Mary to Blackpool, where she abandoned her and escaped. Mary was captured but didn't return to Moor Court.

I hope by this time that she is free and that those, whose lives must have been shattered by the cruel thing she did, have been given the grace to forgive, that their hurt has been healed and that this young woman can begin a new life with a family of her own.

A man on parole

In a previous circuit I had the following experience. It was Sunday morning, I had come home for my lunch and there waiting for me by my garage door was the father of one the older girls in our Youth Club. He waited for me to get out of the car and then came straight for me, looking very angry. "I could b. . . . well kill you" he yelled. I was totally shocked by this and had no idea at all just what had caused this outburst. He soon enlightened me. "You are responsible for that b. . . prisoner coming to our church and mixing with the young people and you never told anyone that he'd been in prison and when he started going out with our S. . . you never warned her the sort of fellow he was."

All this was true. But what happened was this. I had received a 'phone call from a Chaplain in a prison in the South of England who told me that he was trying to help a young prisoner.

"He has no family and has been in prison for six months and his only visitor has been his Probation Officer. He is now due to go out on parole, but we haven't got anywhere at the moment to send him, Would you be able to find him a job perhaps on a farm for a few weeks - and get someone to give him a temporary home?"

He went on to tell me that the Parole Board had unanimously recommended him for parole and that with a bit of encouragement and help he would make a fine young man. I didn't question him any further and I managed to find him a home and a job on a local farm. We welcomed him into our home and he came with us to the local Chapel and was given a warm welcome. The farmer knew that he'd been in prison, but we decided to tell no-one else. He came to the Youth Club and, as he was a good looking young man, wasn't short of admirers and soon found himself a girl friend, who was the daughter of my angry visitor. It happened that he'd been to the local pub and someone had come to him and said, "Did you know that the fellow your S. . . . is going out with is just out of prison?". Well, he didn't know and I don't know who told his informant, but what I do know is that he lost no time in coming to me and telling me, "You can tell that friend of yours if I catch sight of him with my daughter I'll shoot him." He then walked off and I went in for my lunch.

It was later that day, after I had got back from my evening service that this young fellow rang our doorbell. I answered the door and invited him in. He looked terrible. His girl friend had managed to get a message through to him and warned him not to come anywhere near her. He was absolutely devastated. I have never heard anyone cry so bitterly and he went down on his knees crying "Oh God, what shall I do, what shall I do?" The farmer kindly stood by him until he went back to finish his sentence and when he got his release, we managed to help him get a caravan to live in and to get a job as a window cleaner. He did well and bought his own house and settled down, but tragically died prematurely of cancer.

Spiritual Warfare: Exorcism

In this chapter where I share some of my prison experiences, I want to say a brief word about spiritual warfare and exorcism. This is one part of the ministry that I'm very hesitant to talk about. There is a deep mystery about it, and many questions that I can't answer. There is often pain and anguish, and I'm reluctant to get involved. I don't - even if I was able - wish to enter into a deep theological discussion about it, but I do want to make several personal observations.

When a person commits very serious crime that is quite out of character, the question we ask is "Why? What caused them to do this?" The psychologist who studies the mind has important things to say and explanations to give, but, generally speaking, it seems to me that the vast majority rule out the possibility of demonology, and are very scathing about the suggestion that evil powers of darkness might be involved. I know that our understanding of these matters has greatly increased since Jesu's earthly ministry, when a vital part of that ministry was 'casting out demons'. Now in many cases there could have been a psychological explanation, but I'm convinced that - then as now - there are happenings in people's lives and in their homes that can't be given a psychological explanation. There is sometimes a 'something' outside the mind that can attack, and influence the behaviour of a person. That 'something' could be what the Bible calls a devil or a spirit of evil.

C. S. Lewis, "Screwtape Letters"

I find C. S. Lewis's writings often helpful, and his Screwtape Letters, although a work of fiction, is based on certain facts. He says on this matter, "There are two equal opposite errors into which our race can fall, about devils. One is to disbelieve in their existence, and the other is to believe and to take an unhealthy interest in them, They (the devils) are equally pleased by both errors, and they hail a materialist or a magician with the same delight." The Bible has much to say on this subject, but I don't suggest that we all should try on our own to study it. This is a difficult subject, and better left to the specialist. But what I do say is this: - from my experiences as a chaplain in a prison for nine years, and as minister for almost fifty years, that there are some people who behave as they do because an evil spirit has somehow or other gained access into their lives and has had a controlling influence on them; causing them to do evil things, and that their basic need is first and foremost for that evil spirit to be exorcised. When this happens - and it does happen - the results can be spectacular. BUT there is a great need for responsible, balanced and believing people in the church to study this subject, and after careful and prayerful preparation, be made available as Specialists to help in this battle against these evil powers.

CHAPTER FIFTEEN

HOLIDAYS AND HOLY DAYS

All I've seen
Teaches me to trust the creator
For all I've not seen.
Ralph W. Emerson

The family go to Blackpool

My life has been greatly enriched by the holidays that I've had and my memories go back to the time when I was a little lad at Long Lane farm. Then we always went to Blackpool, for father said the air at Blackpool was the best and I think

that he was right. We stayed at a guesthouse called The Worsley, on the front between the Central and North piers. It was self-catering and mother used to fill a huge hamper with food, which included a large cooked chicken, plenty of home-cured bacon and ham, apple pie, cakes and home made biscuits, half a sack of potatoes and carrots. In those early days there would be five of us; father, mother, Herbert, Vera and me. Blackpool seemed such long way then and when we got beyond Preston (there was no M6) father used to tell us to see who could spot Blackpool tower first. The highlight of the holiday was when we all visited the Tower Circus. We spent much time on the lovely golden sands, building our sandcastles and later going in for making racing cars and aeroplanes in sand. It was in those days that the News Chronicle had an advertising gimmick. A man who called himself Mr. Lobby Lud visited various seaside resorts during the summer season, mixing with the crowd. Folk had to buy the paper and then go and try to identify him. Carrying the News Chronicle in their hand, they were required to approach him and say "You are Mr Lobby Lud and I claim the News Chronicle prize", We had great fun trying to identify him when we knew he was at Blackpool, but were even more amused when folk got the idea that father was Mr Lobby Lud and a number challenged him.

Father gives us a blank cheque!

Years later when we went without our parents we stayed at a boarding house - The Grange - and a Mrs Lawrence was the manager. At one time father would book rooms there for a month, Herbert and I had to go at a time to fit in with the corn harvest, usually for two weeks, while he and mother and Vera would go for the other two. I suppose we would be in our late teens when father gave us a blank cheque which we gave to Mrs Lawrence and, instead of carrying much money with us, we would ask her and she gave us what we needed and then added it to the bill. At the time I didn't think much about this, it was simply a convenient way of doing things, but looking back I marvel at the trust involved, both between father and us and between father and Mrs Lawrence.

Happy days!

I often think how fortunate I've been when I compare my life as a late teenager with that of some young folk of the same age today, no job, no hope of a job and surrounded by so many things to do and to buy, but not able to afford them. No wonder they get fed up and rebel and seek ways to escape from the scourge of boredom, by stealing in order to buy drugs and drink, They have my deepest sympathy and I wish that I could have done more to help them, I'm sure of one thing, and that is that the solution to their problem is not simply to lock them up, adding to their boredom.

The Manx TT races

Later, Herbert and I with Arthur Faulkner, Ted Greenway and others went to the Isle of Man for several years for the TT races. We didn't take our own motor bikes, but had plenty of thrills and saw plenty of 'spills', including several serious ones. I remember in particular getting up at 5 am to watch them practising and we were able to go into the stands free at that early hour and see all the activities in the pits as the mechanics got the bikes ready. One morning we watched a young rider getting ready. His girl friend was with him and he gave her a big hug and a kiss and she wished him well. The timekeeper set him off and he went like a rocket roaring out of sight. It was less than ten minutes afterwards we could see that there was great concern in the pit just below us. We didn't know what had happened but it was obvious that they had received some disturbing news. An ambulance went by with its bell ringing. The girl who a few minutes earlier had waved her boy friend off was looking very distraught. Then as we stood there anxiously waiting, news came through that this young fellow had been killed. I'm afraid that we didn't enjoy the races that day and every time I hear of riders getting killed in the Manx TT I think of that scene early in the morning.

Holiday homes and tents

Some of my best holidays have been at our Methodist Guild or Christian Endeavour Holiday Homes. I remember in particular Beechwood Court, Conway and St. Rhadaguands on the Isle of Wight. More recently we have been going to Willersley Castle on the edge of the Peak District, overlooking the River Derwent. Here, in this lovely hotel, our good friends, Carol-Anne and Bill

Eric and Sheila at Willersley Castle

Alcorn are doing a wonderful job as managers, providing excellent facilities for conferences, family holidays and special activity weeks, as well as giving a warm welcome to folk who come on their own and to parties who come for the day.

La Ballena Allegra

While at Alderley Edge we bought a frame tent and went on a most exciting camping holiday in Spain. Two good friends from Alsager - Joyce and Keith Fitzgerald - had been with their two children and persuaded us to join them the following year. This was in 1968 when John was fifteen and Peter eleven.

The holiday was not without incidents. I can think of three in particular.

We had a small Morris twelve, which meant that with four of us, plus all our camping equipment etc. there was not a lot of room to spare. I fastened the tent on a roof rack. While travelling at about 60 mph through France I caught sight in my inside mirror - of something flying through the air. I felt to see if my roof rack was all right and was horrified to discover it had gone, together with the tent. Thankfully very little damage was done to the tent and we managed to get the roof rack mended.

Our second incident was in the centre of Barcelona about 2.30 am. I took a wrong turn and discovered I was going the wrong way in a one way system! A police officer, with a gun on his belt, jumped into the road about two hundred metres ahead of us, waving his arms frantically. We stopped, again we were very

185

fortunate, for at that time there was no other vehicle on the road. The police officer couldn't speak English, but he made it very clear, having looked to see that the way was clear, that he wanted us to make a quick 'U' turn. This we did, and were so thankful to have got away without hurt. I had warned the boys that they would have to behave in Spain as the police carried guns. Peter, on seeing the officer with his arms up, dived to the floor of the car and hid under a rug.

The third incident was following the grandfather of all thunderstorms. I had read about such storms and being a good Scout I was prepared for it and had taken with me a special digging tool (I still have it in my caravan). When we had erected the tent I dug a ditch round it. Our neighbours in the next tent were Germans and they had a son Peter's age called Uve. He and Peter became good friends. Uve's father watched me digging this ditch with great interest.

Bobby Sharlton!

Although Peter didn't know any German and Uve no English, they were able to communicate very well. Peter came to tell us that Uve's parents would like us to go round for a coffee. Sheila took a map of Germany and England, Uve pointed to the town where they lived and we then pointed to Manchester (knowing that Alderley Edge wouldn't mean anything to them), When we mentioned Manchester, immediately Uve said "Bobby Sharlton". Peter managed to explain proudly that Bobby Charlton had been to our home for a meal and that John had played football with him. They were a lovely family and we enjoyed their company.

A good Scout who was prepared

It was a few days later that we had the thunderstorm. In a matter of minutes, very heavy clouds blacked out the sun; it became dark, then the rain came down in torrents. The water rushed through the camp like a river. A man in a nearby tent came floating out on an air-bed and the water swept through Uve's tent, but we escaped for it went round the ditches that I'd dug. Fortunately the hot sun soon dried it up again, Uve's father came round afterwards, pointed to our ditch and gave me a pat on the back. He borrowed my digging tool and dug his ditch and we then lent it to our other neighbours. Happily there were no more thunderstorms and we had a wonderful holiday on that Mediterranean campsite, La Ballena Allegra (The Happy Whale).

Our very own caravan - a holiday home on wheels

One thing that parents soon learn is that their children quickly grow up and want to go away on their own. This happened to us and Sheila and I decided to give up the tent and buy a trailer caravan. Whilst visiting Herbert and Ruth at Tarvin we mentioned this and *IT SO HAPPENED* that, the day before, Ruth's brother and his wife had decided to sell their caravan and buy a bigger one. We had to pass their house on our way home, so we called to have a look at it and fell in love

with it at once. They told us the price - which included an awning and toilet - and we bought it on the spot. That was in 1972 and now twenty-five years later I'm sitting in that same van writing these lines. It was such a thrill to feel that at last we had a little 'home' of our own. We have looked after it carefully over the years, making sure that there were no cracks unfilled and each year we've had the brakes and tyres checked and the underside sealed. We've had some wonderful holidays in it and not once have we come home early because of the weather, or because we weren't enjoying ourselves. These days it's often a talking point amongst our fellow campers and it's nearly always the oldest van on the site. It was a great improvement when our friend Richard Worrall wired it for electrics. We now have a thermostatically controlled heater which keeps us warm and cosy on the coldest of nights.

'Master Chef' uses Dry Fry cooker

I've never had any problem towing the van. Although small it's quite heavy for its size and I can travel at sixty miles an hour and need no stabiliser. We have no water pump or tap, just a couple of plastic containers. Sheila cooks at home and I do the cooking in the van and enjoy doing it. It's very seldom that we eat out, for we both enjoy our home cooking best. We don't have an oven, but instead, all the meat is cooked in a Dry Fry Cooker. This is a great help. It's like a deep frying pan with a lid. However when you remove the lid it reveals that the heat comes through holes in a raised centre (a bit like a small upturned cup without a handle). Anything that we might normally grill is cooked in it. The advantage of this Dry Fry Cooker is that it needs very little gas, using the smallest of flames, There is no smoke and no 'spitting' as with a grill, for the lid prevents this.

Real 'bargain breaks'

One very big advantage of our type of caravan holiday is that it's very much cheaper than staying in a hotel. When we first started, our site fees averaged about 60p per night! Now they average about £6, some sites with electrics being perhaps £10, I suppose it seems that I'm enthusiastic about caravanning; I am,

187

Eric with the caravan at Glen Coe

Sheila with the caravan at Fort William

and so is Sheila, for we enjoy doing the same things and going to the same sort of places. Both of us love walking, especially amongst the mountains in the Lake District or Scotland, or on the coastal paths of Cornwall. Whenever possible we keep away from crowded places. If it's wet there's always plenty to do in the van, reading, writing, crossword puzzles, card games, radio and cassette player (with headphones if only one is listening.) We don't take a television. On Sunday morning we always find a church and enjoy different forms of worship.

Oh Eric, how could you?

I want to end this chapter on holidays by describing two incidents, one that I think of when, in the prayer of confession, we ask for forgiveness for those things we have done that we shouldn't have done.

We were on the Caravan Club site at Meathop, near Grange over Sand. It's a

Eric and Sheila "conquering" Helvellyn

good site with first class facilities, including a rather special exclusive toilet for the disabled, On this occasion our friends Ralph and Barbara Thorley and Janet and Margaret Hodgson were next to us on the site and Ralph and Barbara had come round to our van for a chat. I went across to the toilet-block, which was quite near and as there was no one else in decided I would look at and use the toilet for the disabled. I hadn't been in long when two men came, one helping the other and tried the door. When they discovered it was locked one said angrily "I bet it's somebody in there who isn't disabled." I felt very guilty and when I had finished doing what I went in to do, on the spur of the moment decided to act as though I was disabled, without reckoning on what complications might follow. So I slowly opened the door and struggled out, walking with my right leg straight and toe turned in and my whole body twisted. They spoke kindly to me and the disabled man went in and his helper watched me go; no doubt, because of what he had said, feeling a bit guilty as I struggled out. As I made my 'painful' way across to our van, Ralph saw me coming and was horrified and exclaimed "I'm afraid there is something seriously wrong with Eric." Sheila came running to me. "Whatever is the matter?" she cried. I said "Let me get into the van and I'll tell you." When I did tell them, they didn't know whether to laugh or give me a good telling off. One thing that they did decide was that I would have to stay in the van, as long as I was 'disabled'. It was fortunate that the man and his friend left later that day and I was able to have a 'miraculous recovery'. I've told that story many times and we've had many laughs, but I did wrong and I wont do it again.

Almost a reluctant streaker

This is a story about something that nearly happened, and every time I think about it I get shivers up my spine. On this occasion we were at one of our favourite sites - Skelwith Fold in the Lake District, near Ambleside. I went across for a shower and it was one where money was put into a slot machine on the door, before you could get into the shower cubicle. I went in, shut the door, got undressed and turned the water on and discovered that the outlet plughole was blocked with matted hair etc. and the water couldn't get away. I removed the messy stuff and decided that the best place to put it was in the waste bin and that was outside the cubicle, about three feet away. I was the only person in the toilet block at that time, so I opened the door and made a quick dash in the nude to the waste bin. The door, which was on a spring, began to close quickly behind me. In a flash I kicked out with my foot at the closing door and just managed to put my toe in it and prevent it from closing on me. In a split second I would have been locked out with nothing on and no money to open the door to get to my clothes.

I had a nightmare that night thinking about it and trying to imagine just what Sheila would have thought if I'd been a 'streaker'.

"Some mothers do 'ave 'em!".

Holy Days

The best holiday of my life began like this: I was sitting at my desk, when the 'phone rang. It was Stanley Johnson, the minister from Longton Central Hall and a very good friend. "How would you like to come with me as a joint party leader to the Holy Land next Easter for fifteen days?" When I got over the initial surprise I said "Very much, but tell me more." He then went on to say that he had got a good party from the Central Hall who had booked and that if I could get about a dozen more from the Cheadle circuit and was willing to share the leadership with him, I could go free. I told him that I'd always wanted to go to the Holy Land and this was a wonderful opportunity. I wanted Sheila to come too, but at that time her mother was living with us and wasn't well and she didn't feel she could leave her. This was a big disappointment but she encouraged me to go. There were forty of us in the party and we went by coach to Heath Row and flew by Jumbo Jet to Tel Aviv then by coach to the President Hotel in Jerusalem. The journey was not without incident! In the first place Amy Goodwin, a most loveable little lady, left her handbag in the toilet at Heath Row with her flight ticket, money and passport in it. She panicked but we managed to get it back just in time. Then as the plane roared across the runway gathering speed ready for take off, the pilot suddenly jammed on his brakes, threw us all forward and this huge plane with its four hundred and more passengers aboard came to a sudden standstill. The pilot apologised and said that there was a 'technical hitch' and that we would all have to disembark, taking our hand luggage with us. We were shepherded into one of the main lounges and through the window could see staff quickly removing all our luggage. What was wrong? It seemed that just as we were about to take off a coded warning had been sent to say that there was a bomb on board in someone's luggage! It was a false alarm but it meant we were eight hours late leaving. Our troubles, however, weren't over, for when we at last arrived at Tel Aviv and waited for our luggage to come round on the carousel, we discovered that our bags had been opened and several - including mine - hadn't been fastened properly. I could see my pyjama trousers going round! But we were the lucky ones, for six passengers discovered that their luggage was missing. Stanley and I had our work cut out helping to comfort and taking practical steps to put matters right. A 'phone call through to Heath Row confirmed that the missing cases were there and would arrive early the next day and be delivered to our hotel. It was the early hours of the morning when we set off for Jerusalem and we arrived at our hotel a bit travel weary. But then began - for me at any rate - a fantastic experience. We were on a pilgrimage and I was excited, for we were going to walk where Jesus walked, see things that Jesus saw and perhaps even touch something that he had actually touched. I took many photographs and had my tape recorder with me and recorded many of the sounds. Now come with me as we make our pilgrimage in this Holy Land.

Where shepherds watched their flocks by night

We had three different guides. Our first was an Arab, Freddie, a lovely fellow and most helpful. He knew the Scriptures and made the Bible stories live. We began in Bethlehem 'where shepherds watched their flock by night' and then we walked over the shepherds' field and down into Bethlehem itself. Here little Freddie reminded us that Ruth met Boaz in one of the fields close by and David himself was born here and of course, Jesus. We went into the church of the Holy Nativity built over the stable and inn where Jesus was born. This was most ornate and a huge golden star marked the spot where the manger was reputed to have been.

Jerusalem

Now we go back to Jerusalem. It's a wonderful city, unique amongst the cities of the world and is the most sacred city for almost half the human race.

For the Jews, first and foremost this is the city of David. The city where Solomon built his wonderful temple. Here is enshrined their past glory and future hope.

For Christians this is the city of Jesus - the place where he worshipped, wept, died and on the third day rose again. Here the Christian church was born.

For the Muslims this is the city to which Mohammed came, and from which it's believed he went up into heaven.

Freddie informed us that Jerusalem was then (1977) the home of some 215,000 Jews and 85,000 Arabs. It's a city that is 'high and lifted up' being built on four hills. The one building whose dome stands out is the Dome of the Rock. This great dome is made of aluminium bronze and is 180 feet high, a real landmark that shines bright, towering over the city and built over the rock where Abraham came to offer his son Isaac. It was here that King Solomon built the original

The Dome of the Rock, Jerusalem

temple and it was to this same rock that Mohammed came. We all had to take our shoes off before entering and left them outside. Freddie assured us that he had never heard of anyone's shoes being stolen. Inside was the most beautiful carpet presented by the late Shah of Persia. Close by was the Wailing Wall, or as the Jews call it, the Western Wall. This is the holiest shrine of the Jewish world. Its base was part of the wall that surrounded the Temple and was spared by Titus in the year AD 70. Each block of stone was huge. Down through the years Jews have come to the wall to pray, however from 1948 to 1967 they were not allowed to come for it was then in the Jordanian section of the city. After the Six-Day War in June 1967 it was recaptured and has become a place of national rejoicing as well as a place for worshippers. While we were there it was the anniversary of the Six-Day War and we joined in the celebrations in St. David's Park. It was a most moving experience, I've never seen such joy on the faces of people as they danced and clapped. Everyone was so jolly and friendly. At one point I was surrounded by half a dozen lovely Jewish girls, each having a kind of plastic hammer which squeaked as they hit me on the head. It was all good fun.

The last days in the life of Jesus

The next part of our pilgrimage took us to places visited by Jesus as he came to the end of his earthly ministry.

I wanted to linger long in the Garden of Gethsemane, this sacred place, at the foot of the Mount of Olives. Freddie told us that it had been preserved over the centuries and that botanists claim that the trees - some of them - could be three thousand years old and if they were, and had managed to escape the destruction of Jerusalem in AD70, then they could be the very trees that had stood there as Jesus prayed in agony of soul, just before He was arrested. He knew that He was going to face the most cruel of deaths by being nailed to a cross of wood and left hanging till he died. No wonder that He prayed, "Father, if it be possible let this cup pass from me; nevertheless, not as I will, but as thou wilt." When I read these words now, my thoughts take me to that sacred garden.

192

We were then taken up the stone steps where Jesus was taken after His arrest, to the house of Caiaphas, the High priest. This was where Peter denied three times that he knew Jesus, and then hearing a cock crow, remembered that Jesus had said, "Peter, before the cock crows you will say three times that you do not know me". When he remembered, he went out and wept bitterly. As Freddie recalled these events, I don't think there was a dry eye amongst us. Many of these places made sacred by what happened there, now have a church covering the place. The church built over this place is called 'St. Peter in Gallicantu' where Peter heard the cock crow. From there we went to the place where the trial had been held and then to the dungeons beneath where Jesus was scourged (whipped with long leather thongs in which sharp pieces of rock or bone had been implanted) and then had salt rubbed into His bleeding back. I will never forget that place.

From there we walked the VIA DOLOROSA, 'The Way of the Cross', the way that Jesus had walked after being condemned to death by Pilate. On this way there are fourteen 'stations', at each there is an ornate chapel, marking the spot where some incident took place on that painful journey, There is one, for example, where Jesus fell, unable to carry that heavy cross any further and where Simon, a black man from N. Africa who was amongst the crowd was forced to carry it for Him. Now, the Via Dolorosa is a very busy narrow shopping street and these 'stations' would have been lost but for the chapels that have been built. Each Friday a group of monks known as 'The Little White Fathers' walk this way carrying a cross and stopping at each station to say prayers. The road leads to Calvary, 'The Place of the Skull', and when you look at this hill you know why it was so named. There we bowed our heads and then sang:

> *There is a green hill far away,*
> *Outside a city wall,*
> *Where the dear Lord was crucified*
> *Who died to save us all*

Easter joy

Close by the 'Place of the Skull' there is the garden of Joseph of Arimathea, in which was the tomb where they buried Jesus, sealing it with a great stone. It was here where the women came on that first Easter day and discovered that the stone had been moved and that Jesus had risen. It was Easter when we were there and we had a wonderful service of Holy Communion when we sang some joyful Easter hymns.

Now on to Galilee

We were then going to leave Jerusalem and make our way to Galilee, a journey that Jesus must have done many times, but he walked and we went by coach. But first we went to Jericho. I wouldn't have liked to walk that road alone. It's easy to understand why Jesus made this road the setting for one of his best loved stories - that of the Good Samaritan. We then had a Jewish guide - not nearly so good as

Freddie - and he pointed to an Inn on that journey and said that it was built on the site of the one where the Good Samaritan took the poor man. When we reminded him that it was only a story, he said it was a story based on fact and tradition has it that this is 'The Inn of the Good Samaritan'. We didn't argue.

Massada

Our place of special interest on this journey was Massada, a mountain stronghold just two and a half miles from the Dead Sea. This place has become a shrine for the Jewish people, because it's the site of one of the most dramatic episodes in their history. We went to the top by cable car on a very hot day. It was just like being in a hot oven. Some of our party had stopped to bathe in the Dead Sea - what a sea! It's 47 miles long and 10 wide and is in fact 1,290 feet below sea level and 1,278 feet deep. It's the lowest spot on the earth's surface. Seven million tons of water flow into it every day, but there is no outlet - it all evaporates. It's called 'dead' because nothing can live in it. Those who bathed in it could float, but they came out very sticky. Not a place to stay.

Zacceaus, come down, today I am coming to your house

From the Dead Sea we made our way to Jericho, reputed to be the oldest town in the world and set in a wonderful oasis, where they grew the most luscious oranges. Yes, there was a huge sycamore tree there too, just to remind us of the day when that chief tax collector, who had spent his life making money, had climbed up a sycamore tree in order to see Jesus. How I wish that we could have met this little man there and heard from his own lips his story of how he met Jesus and the difference that it made in his life.

Galilee

On to the town of Tiberias where we were to spend a whole week close to the Sea of Galilee. It's not a sea really, more of an inland lake just thirteen miles long and seven across and the water is fresh. It's also called Lake Tiberias. Jesus spent many days on or around this lake and here we relaxed. We swam in it; we sailed across it; we held an open-air service on its shores and picnicked where Jesus had breakfast with Peter and the other fishermen. On our last evening we watched a most wonderful sunset, as Jesus must have done many times. Somehow we felt that He was watching with us. This was an unforgettable holiday, for these were indeed HOLY DAYS.

CHAPTER SIXTEEN

RE-TYRED!

Prayer not only makes a difference,
Prayer makes all the difference.   Billy Graham

Supernumerary - surplus to requirements!

I've enjoyed my life as a minister and had many memorable experiences, some that I've written about in this book.

One that stands out now as I look back, was the "Farewell Social" that the circuit arranged for me to mark my retirement. I had mixed feelings about this. In a way I felt sad, for I loved the job God gave me to do and had found great satisfaction in it and this meeting would mark the time when I would become a Supernumerary minister.

One meaning of the word is 'one who is surplus to requirements'. This gave me the feeling that now I was becoming a 'has been'. On the other hand, I was very much looking forward to being relieved of the chores of a Superintendent minister . . . all the admin. work, dealing with finance and property matters. I know that they're very important, but I felt that my priority was that of caring for people, preaching and encouraging those working with young people. I also knew that amongst the congregations there were those who were much more capable of dealing with these other matters than I was and where possible I had made full use of them,

Our Farewell Social

Why then was this Farewell Social so memorable? Both Sheila and I were feeling very sad about leaving Cheadle, having been there for ten years and made so many good friends. For our final week-end they had arranged a Flower Festival, in addition to the Farewell Social.

Representatives of the different churches under my care were to take part and at some stage I would have an opportunity to give my 'Swan song', I was wishing that some of my family could have been there. Peter, who'd come to see us just prior to his going back to the Sudan to teach for a second year, had gone to stay with John in Macclesfield the night before. I 'phoned John and Fiona and invited them to come, but they were most apologetic, saying that they had a long standing engagement and that Peter was invited also. Then I 'phoned my eldest brother Wilfred and he, too, reported that he and Mary had an engagement, which also included my sister Vera and Douglas. It was now late on the Friday night and Sheila discouraged me from doing any more 'phoning. Next morning, feeling very sad, I shut myself away from everyone in the caravan and prepared my final messages.

Sheila and I went down to the Flower Festival in the afternoon and were most impressed. A lot of people from far and wide came. When we returned in the evening we were welcomed by the chairman, Bob Richards and taken to a seat on the front row of the crowded church hall. Bob introduced the various concert items which ended with a humorous poem about us recited by Christina Withers, who'd been so very helpful to me. I thought that Christina's poem was the final item. Sheila was then presented with a bouquet and I received a cheque and got up to thank everyone.

"Eric Challoner, This is Your Life"

I was just getting 'launched' when Bill Mosley, a Local Preacher and Leader, left his seat and came straight for me and took hold of my arm very firmly as I was talking and in a loud voice cried "ERIC CHALLONER, THIS IS YOUR LIFE". He was carrying a big red book, At that moment the stage curtains were drawn back revealing a lovely floral background and a large circle of empty chairs and Sheila and I were escorted on to the stage. Bill then began to read from the big red book.

The first thing he said was "Members of your family are here tonight to join you and Sheila", then on to the stage walked John and Fiona, followed by Peter, all 'laughing their heads off'. What a lovely surprise. They were followed by Wilfred and Mary, Herbert and Ruth and Vera and Douglas. As I gave them all a

Vera, Mary, Wilfred, Ruth, Eric, Sheila & Herbert

196

warm handshake and hug, a big lump came into my throat. I turned to Sheila and said "Did you know anything about this?" She just gave me a big smile. Then Bill went on to say, "We don't forget your brother Walter who died in November 1937, leaving behind a widow Edna - and two little daughters. Your sister-in-law now lives in Australia with her elder daughter Daphne." At that moment the voices of Edna and Daphne came over on the PA system loud and clear and I thought for a moment they had flown over, but it was a lovely recorded message, Then Bill step by step told my life story. As it unfolded some of the very good

friends who were part of that story came on the stage; some of whom I hadn't seen for years, but at some stage of my life had a vital part to play. There were those who had come not only as friends, but representing the different churches where I had ministered. There were others who weren't able to come but who sent their greetings by letter or tape. I was completely overwhelmed. It was without doubt the biggest surprise of my life and I just marvelled how Sheila had masterminded it all and had done it without my knowing a thing about it. Lots of folk said to me afterwards, "Surely you must have suspected something." I can honestly say that I didn't.

One of my most prized possessions is the big red book that was composed by Sheila and beautifully produced by our artistic friend Richard Taylor. We later received two beautiful albums of photographs taken during that evening by another good friend, Ken Bradshaw. The next day I conducted my final services, and on the following Wednesday we left Cheadle for our new home in Alsager. Peter was with us and helped with the move. On the way to Alsager we took him to Crewe Station, where he began his journey to the Sudan, Good friends were waiting for us at No. 31 and so began a new chapter in our lives.

The pain of moving

In the opening pages of this book I wrote of the pain I felt as a lad when we moved from Long Lane farm, Over Peover, to the New Pale, Manley; and the difficulties that father had as a farmer, The minister has special problems, too, when he moves. He is not simply leaving a job, but leaving his people, with whom he had forged a close bond, sharing their times of both joy and sadness. Our move from Cheadle was better than most because we were moving to a place where we already had friends, and to a house that for the first time was our very own. We didn't have to face a series of welcome meetings, or start preparing services for the following Sunday. We were free! Free to go where we wanted to go and free to worship together.

My next assignment??

I've already said that I didn't like the word supernumerary 'surplus to requirements'. Neither, as a minister, do I like the word retirement. At 65 I still had a mission to fulfil. But just what was that mission to be? All ministers today are allowed to have a sabbatical every seven years. For three months they are relieved of their ministerial duties, while they relax, take stock of their lives and make a study of some subject that might help them in their work. I'd never had a sabbatical, so I decided to have one when I retired and during that period to seek guidance concerning my future mission.

Billy Graham Comes to Anfield

The weeks and months flew and it was now 1984. I began taking a limited number of preaching appointments. One Monday in February, Sheila and I were invited to a meeting in a neighbouring village. This was a preparation meeting for the Billy Graham Mission. The leader was Barbara Jones, an Anglican lady from Audley, who gave a lively account of what was going on in the various churches in the area and especially of the growing interest in the Billy Graham Crusade. I was very surprised to hear this, for I'd not heard of anyone in Alsager who was interested and I had my own doubts about this sort of campaign. Barbara had put up a large map of the Potteries area and this map was covered with small flags placed round individual churches, each flag representing a Prayer Triplet - a group of three people meeting together regularly to pray. Some of the churches were surrounded by flags but in spite of the fact that there were seven churches in Alsager there was only one flag.

In that meeting I became aware that I had to do something about this. I shared my concern with the Council of Churches who agreed to arrange a Prayer seminar and invited Barbara Jones to speak. 25 people attended and I was appointed Prayer Co-ordinator for Alsager. Barbara suggested that individuals from different churches might like to meet; just two at first and then they together invite a third to join them.

My Prayer Partner Roy

At that meeting I met Roy Pitcher, a senior lecturer at the Crewe and Alsager College of Higher Education (now Manchester Metropolitan University). He was very enthusiastic about the suggestions and asked me to be his prayer partner.

We agreed to meet at 6.30 am each Thursday. That was in 1984 and we've continued to meet every week since, except holiday times, or when Roy - who is now an Ofsted inspector - is on one of his school inspections. The question that I'm often asked is "Does prayer really make a difference?" This is something that's not easy to prove, but all that I know is that many things have happened in my life that I'm convinced wouldn't have happened without prayer. I've already mentioned some in this book. Here's another.

A free ride to Anfield. But who's going to pay?

In the early days of our prayer partnership, Roy and I concentrated our prayers on the forthcoming Billy Graham Campaign to be held at Anfield, Liverpool's famous football stadium. I told him that Sheila and I were planning to be responsible for one coach and that we had asked Alwyn Gilbertson, a Christian friend who acted as a local agent for Bostock's Coaches, to book it. Roy promised to help fill it. In spite of the fact that we were finding great difficulty in filling the one coach, as we prayed one morning it became very clear that instead of having just one we should have eight, one for every night of the campaign. When we told Alwyn he thought we were making a terrible mistake. "Do you realise" he said "that these coaches are going to cost seventy pounds each, and if you don't fill them you'll still have to pay the full amount?" Roy and I still felt that we should take a big step of faith and confirm the bookings. Poor Alwyn - he just couldn't believe it. "How much am I to charge?" he anxiously asked. I must say that at this time the response was not very encouraging and the nagging thought kept coming that we ought to listen to Alwyn. But we had ordered the coaches because we firmly believed that this was what God wanted us to do. What was wrong? We had too little faith. We must let every one go free and simply take a thank-offering on the way home! This seemed a crazy idea, but this is exactly what we did. In the meantime, Roy arranged for us to have 5000 leaflets printed and every household had one. We got in touch with the Billy Graham team in Liverpool and they arranged for two young men to come and speak at the local Comprehensive School Assembly. The coaches were filled.

The coaches were paid for. Each driver was given a £7.50 tip. And we had a surplus of £347, which we distributed to mission projects, both local and national.

Days of decision at Anfield

Those were memorable evenings. It was a tremendous thrill to see that great stadium filled to overflowing with thousands of people, young and old, joining with the great Crusade choir in the singing and then to listen to Billy Graham. He had that wonderful gift of communication which enabled him to make each person there feel that he was talking to them directly. Every night he began by making us all laugh and then he reminded us of the world as it's and the mess we are making of it, as a nation and as individuals. He nearly always referred to some item on the latest news bulletin to illustrate this. Then came a picture of the world as God meant it to be, and as it could be; if only we changed our ways to His way - the way of Christ.

"This day for you is a day of decision, turn to Christ" was his nightly challenge. There was no emotional appeal, no pleading, Like a skilled barrister, he put his case, the verdict was in each individual's hands. I had persuaded a neighbour to go - a Professor of Philosophy at the College and a declared atheist, a writer of several books and a broadcaster. He was most surprised on two counts. First, by Billy Graham's simple message without the histrionics that he had expected. But most of all by the fact that hundreds of people, both young and old, quietly left their seats and walked (quite a long way for some) across the precious green turf of Anfield towards the platform, "I just can't account for that - it's a complete mystery to me", was his comment as we travelled home on the coach. There was an 'element' there that he didn't understand; a spiritual element that he hadn't discovered, in spite of his great learning. I explained that for months prayer had been focussed on that Crusade. Everyone who walked forward, most probably had been prayed for by someone. This was a vital part of that Campaign and Billy Graham would add, " . . . the most vital part, for prayer not only makes a difference, but makes all the difference."

PROBUS

One of the best things that I've done since retiring has been to join Probus. This is a Club for retired professional and business men which meets once a month for lunch, It includes bank managers, college lecturers, lawyers, council officials, leaders from industry and commerce, etc. Our membership is limited to sixty and has a waiting list. It's a very interesting group of men, many of whom have no church connections. It's non-religious, non-political and non-sectarian and opened up for me a new sphere of service. Without being officially appointed they've come to regard me as their chaplain. With a group of men whose average age must be seventy, there's always someone sick at home or in hospital and I visit them. I've been a member now for over fourteen years, during which time a number of men have died. I've shared in some of their funeral services and I keep in touch with Probus widows. At each meeting the President welcomes everybody and then calls on me to report on the state of the sick and to say grace before our meal. My favourite grace is:

For love in a world where there is so much hatred,
For friends in a world where there is so much loneliness,
For food in a world where there is so much hunger,
We give to You, O Lord, our most grateful thanks.

It was a great joy to me when I was invited to become their vice President, prior to my becoming President. I felt very honoured. At that time the President was Bert Maxfield. He was a lovely fellow and Bert and I became good friends. We meet on the second Tuesday of every month at noon, in the tap-room of the 'Thirteen Club'. Bert would always buy me a drink, but could never understand why I wouldn't have an alcoholic drink and instead asked for a ginger beer or orange juice. The barman knew what I had, so when Bert shouted to him "Give Eric his whisky and soda", he gave me my ginger beer. Although Bert joked about it, he wasn't happy and told me so. I told him that all through my ministry I had faced this problem and that it hadn't been an easy one to resolve. I acknowledged the fact that generally speaking the local pub was a place of hospitality, providing companionship for people who are lonely. I agreed also that a bottle or two of wine can be a good means of enlivening a party or enriching a friendship. In face of this, why then did I decide not to drink alcohol? The answer can be summed up in just three words because I believe that DRINK IS DANGEROUS, and millions have been spent by the big brewers to hide this fact and to create an image of the man who is teetotal as a man who is weak, a spoil sport and a loser. In contrast, they spend millions to equate the man who drinks, with the sportsman, a man who is a hero, a winner. Statistics tell a grim story to illustrate the fact that drink is dangerous.

On the eight o'clock news this morning there was a report issued by the European Transport Commission's President Mr Neil Kinnock. It stated that in the forty days since the tragic death of Diana, Princess of Wales, four thousand people had been killed, like her, in drink related road accidents; an average of one hundred every day. Only people who have had loved ones killed in such accidents can appreciate the real significance of these statistics. In moderation drink does contribute to enriching the lives of many people and I admit that and would be very much against prohibiting it, but I would prohibit the blatant advertising that hides the fact that it can turn sensible young people into vandals and car drivers into killers. Having discussed this matter with Bert he understood my attitude to drink and respected it.

Prostate procrastination

As chaplain of Probus, I discovered that many of the members at one time or another had a Prostate problem, so I wasn't surprised when my 'water works' weren't functioning properly. I now give a calendar of events, including my first visit to the doctor about this matter.

30.9.94 Doctor informs me I need to see Urologist

11.10.94 I receive a letter from Mr Liu to say it will be twenty six weeks before he is able to see me.

17.5.95 (thirty two weeks later) I went to the Urology clinic and was given a thorough examination by Mr Liu's assistant. He told me that I had the biggest prostate that he had ever felt and it most probably meant that I would have to have major surgery

9.6.95 I had a Pelvic Scan,

5.10.95 I went again to the clinic for a 'Free Flow' test. Then I saw Mr Liu himself, who had the result of my tests and confirmed that I needed an operation. I was asked to report to ward 105 at the City General on 5th December ready for my operation the next day. That was on the 5th of October.

On 16th of November, Sheila went to the doctor thinking she had a bowel problem. He gave her a quick examination and discovered an ovarian lump and arranged for her to see a consultant the next day. He confirmed the GP's diagnosis and said he wanted her in as soon as possible. Due to a cancellation she was asked to report to ward 103 on December 6th, the day after I was due in! I'll never forget that fortnight. I'd been living under the shadow of the big 'C' and Sheila had been comforting me. Now we both faced major surgery and didn't know just what the outcome would be. We did our best to put our affairs in order and to arrange for good neighbours and friends to look after the house, the incoming mail and to deal with the many enquiries. We also had to think about post-hospital care, for I had been expecting Sheila to look after me.

On December 5th 1995, Sheila and a friend took me into hospital, but after having all my pre-op tests I was informed that there was no bed for me and I must go home and report back the next morning. Under ordinary circumstances I would have been upset by this but it now meant that we could go in together.

However, later that evening I received word from the sister on ward 105 telling me not to come in until they sent for me. I took Sheila in at 11 am, made sure that there was a bed for her and then went round toward 105, to see when a bed might be available for me. No one could tell me. On the side of the reception desk there was a huge flower arrangement, with a card on which was written, "To the Rev.

Eric Challoner, With Love from John, Fiona, Ben and Kate." I suggested taking it to ward 103 for Sheila, but she'd already got one from John and family, so I took mine home. Sheila had her operation the next day and made a good recovery. I was kept busy at home and kept a record of all 'phone calls and callers (there were 135 while she was in). It was a great comfort to have so many friends who were concerned enough to enquire. She was out in five days and I was able, with help of a host of very kind friends, to care for her.

In the meantime, my problem hadn't gone away and I was getting worse each day, so I was very relieved to get a message from Mr Liu's secretary asking me to report to ward 105 on the 25th of January ready for my operation on the 26th. I went through all the pre-op. tests as before, which took the best part of three hours, then went into the waiting room to WAIT FOR MY BED. The young doctor came in and said "Mr Challoner, I'm afraid there is no bed at the moment. Will you go home and give us a ring in the morning?" I just couldn't believe it. It was no use arguing or being angry. I went home, phoned at 7.45 the next morning and was told "Come in and we'll do our best." I arrived at the hospital at 8.40 and was given a bed and told I was first on the list. While I was putting on my white stockings and theatre gown the trolley arrived to take me. I climbed on it and was off. It was like a dream after all the waiting. I must say as I was being wheeled down I felt a deep peace. In fact it was more; it was a deep sense of JOY. Looking back, I would say that it was one of my richest and most significant spiritual experiences. I felt the presence of God in a wonderful way. At that time I knew that Sheila was praying for me and my good friend Frank Robbins (who is now in heaven) and a number of other friends. Their prayers were answered. I had the op. and was home again in less than a week and this is a copy of the letter that I sent.

"To all the staff on 105,

I'm so very thankful to you all for your love and care during my stay in 105 I was most impressed by the relaxed and friendly atmosphere in the ward and also by the team-work displayed. It was good to see the professional way the different 'shifts' took over and also the way individuals showed real compassion and care. I will remember you all with gratitude, During my stay, my critical attitude to the hospital system changed, as I saw the problems faced and the way they were met. In the six bed bay in 105 that I was in, for instance, I came to realise that it was quite impossible to say in the morning how many of those beds would be available by the evening. I do not know how many bed patients there were in the hospital, but each of us had our own individual menu for breakfast, lunch and evening meal. Each meal meant to be hot, was hot, and we couldn't only choose what to have, but how much. I came full of criticism; I left full of praise and understanding."

Looking back over this sequence of events, it's quite remarkable that *IT SO HAPPENED* that my operation was postponed for six weeks - just the time

Sheila needed to recover and then take care of me. And what was most important, our biopsies were both benign.

Another prayer adventure

One morning Roy arrived very disturbed by something that he had read. It was a UNICEF report in which it was estimated that 15 million boys and girls die before the age of 5 in the so called developing countries every year and safe water and good sanitation could save half of these. We thought of the pain and anguish that the death of just one of those little ones would cause - but 15 million - every year!

This was a staggering statement, and there was the temptation that because the problem was so great and our resources so limited the little that we could do would make very little difference. However we began to pray about it, and it was then that Roy had this vision of launching a Community Project for Alsager.

There was already a well-established Save the Children Committee in Alsager and we joined them and decided to focus our attention on the Tonga people living in the Zambezi Valley in Zimbabwe. These people had lost their homes following the creation of Lake Kariba in 1960, and had been moved to an area where the land was poor and the water was very scarce. These people were suffering and their little ones were dying. Save the Children had already got a project going in this area, and the more we read about it the more keen we became to support it.

The people they were helping were encouraged to help themselves. Before help was given the villagers were consulted, making sure that the wells would be dug in the best places. Local people were employed in making roads, and providing basic material such as rock and sand. When a well was dug three members of the digging team were drawn from the village community. Once completed, a village water and sanitation committee was set up,

The vision that we had was to get the whole community of Alsager involved. A 6 month Community Project was launched. We knew that it was vital first of all to educate the people to the need. Local ministers became involved, several of us visited the schools and the local Council was most helpful, and the Clerk, Ann Hurlstone was inspired to write a message in song based on our slogan:

TO AFRICA FROM ALSAGER WITH LOVE

There was a catchy tune and here is one verse and chorus:

"We want to show we care through our prayers and through our giving,
By sending what we can to make your life worth living.
May you go from strength to strength as other countries send relief
May you know the love of Jesus, and a certain sure belief
        Chorus
        He'll give you love,
        He'll give you Joy,

Hope to every man and woman,
Hope to every girl and boy.
We are guided in our actions by our Saviour from above
And from Alsager to Africa,
WE SEND YOU LOVE."

A Singing Group made a recording and churches used it in their services and schools in their Assemblies, and with the very lively tune it became popular.

Roy estimated that over 2,000 people had shared in this project, and when the Campaign got going our Save the Children Treasurer Beryl Fuller, with her husband Rex, (now sadly deceased) was receiving £500 a week, much of it collected in family jam jars.

A Royal visitor flies in.

The climax came when Princess Anne arrived in her Royal Helicopter to collect the cheque for £18,000. Roy greeted her and thanked her for coming. She inspected the display that had been prepared in the Alsager College Hall, and spoke to the different groups of helpers who were assembled round the hall, Sheila and I were there with the local clergy. She asked me what the churches had done: I told her and then introduced the local clergy to her. It was a great joy to see the way the whole community of Alsager had been united by this effort; churches and schools; church members and non-members; old and young all working together,

You may ask "Did your prayers make any difference? Did God do what you asked him to do?" My answer to that is that in our prayers we didn't give God His

instructions; telling Him what we wanted Him to do, but having had a vision of the need, together we waited on God to know what He wanted us to do, and asked for His guidance.

To Africa from Alsager with love
1991 ~ 92

TO

THE PRINCESS ROYAL

Thank you for coming to receive Alsager's Community Life Project's expression of good will and our desire to help the people of Zimbabwe to have a reliable water supply.

 Changing ....
Cries for Help .... to .... Shouts of Joy!!

CHAPTER SEVENTEEN

FAMILY

All I have needed thy hand has provided,
Great is thy faithfulness, Lord unto me.
                                    Thomas O. Chisholme

John and Peter

Looking back over the years we have happy memories of both our boys - now men, and I want to include in this final chapter a special word about them,

How quickly they've grown. I'm glad that when they were young I had a tape recorder and we have several hours of recordings that they made in their very early years. Sheila and I treasure those tapes and have had many nostalgic moments listening. Both loved to sing and had a good ear for music and at an early age could sing in tune and also recite. I wish that we'd had a camcorder to accompany those tapes. One of John's favourite pieces that he recited when he was about five (after which he would laugh heartily) was:-

> *I know a man who always wore a saucepan on his head,*
> *I asked him what he did it for,*
> *"I don't know why" he said,*
> *"It always makes my ears so sore.*
> *I am a foolish man,*
> *I should have left it off before and worn a frying pan."*

We have several recordings of his parties, when he and the guests had a concert amongst themselves, each giving their 'party piece'. There was much talent revealed, and they enjoyed entertaining themselves. It's difficult for our grandchildren to imagine life without television, but at that time they provided their own entertainment, I'm sure that they enjoyed themselves more and were less bored than many young people today. John composed the following poem:

IN THE DENTIST'S WAITING ROOM

> *The awful moment looms ahead,*
> *The moment which we all so dread.*
> *We turn the pages of a book,*
> *But at the words we do not look.*
> *I look around the room and see*
> *Others in a state like me,*

They chew their nails and tap their feet,
Fidget and wriggle in their seat
The smart assistant opens the door and says,
"We're ready for Mrs Moore."
She's glad her turn has come at last,
Her time of waiting now is past
The rest of us still paler grow
And wonder who's the next to go.
We think "Why ever did we come?
The pain has gone now from our gum."
But when we reach the dentist's chair,
We find that we no longer care.
The ordeal's over, tooth is out,
Whatever did we fuss about?

John Challoner (aged 13)

Peter wants a dog

Peter was two and a half when we moved to Alsager and the one thing that he
wanted was a little dog. Whilst both Sheila and I love dogs, we'd decided that we
wouldn't have one, for several reasons. As well as needing a lot of care and
attention, we felt that a dog in a manse where we had so many visitors and
meetings wasn't a good idea. So we tried to dissuade him. However, each night,
at the end of his prayers he put in a special petition, "Please, Lord Jesus, let me
have a little dog". When I told my mother about this, her reply was "When you
were Peter's age, you had a dog, a rabbit, some little ferrets and at times, a pet
lamb, I think he ought at least to have a dog." "But mother," I replied, "that was
on the farm". She still persisted and at last we agreed, so she bought him one and
I went and collected it one night, after Peter had gone to bed. We hadn't told
him, thinking it would be a lovely surprise. The next morning, the little pup (and
it was very little) was lying curled up in its basket, by the fireside, fast asleep.
Peter came down in his pyjamas, saw it lying there, and thought that it was a toy
dog. I'll never forget that moment when he discovered that it was real. He picked
it up and shouted "Daddy, it's alive." Although he was still in his pyjamas and
dressing gown, he insisted on taking it for a walk there and then around the
garden. When he came in, we told him to think of a name. Without any hesitation
he said "Pongo". This was the name of a dog that Sheila had when she was young
and he must have heard her mention its name.

Pongo, The Manse Guard Dog

For over seventeen years Pongo was a very important member of the Challoner
household. We all loved him (most of the time) in spite of the fact that he chased
every cat, fought with every dog (size didn't matter to Pongo), attacked the post
man, the dust men and even our very good friend Harry Potts when he delivered

the groceries. Correction, he didn't attack him when he delivered, but when he picked up the empty box to take back . . . I believe that if we could have studied why he did what he did, we would discover that he believed that he had a vital role to play in our family. He was the Manse Guard Dog, and his job was to protect us from all intruders, whether man or beast who stepped on to his territory. He must have been very hurt when I shouted at him.

We were all very sad when he died. It was Boxing Day and one of the rare occasions when John and Peter were both at home together. They dug a grave in the rose garden at the manse at Cheadle, and I offered a short prayer of thanksgiving for our brave little Manse Guard Dog as we 'laid him to rest' in his basket.

John: Lawyer and International Tax Consultant

Both of our sons went to University; John to Exeter and Peter to Newcastle-on-Tyne. Both managed to get their degrees, John in Law and Peter in English Literature. After finishing his Articles with our solicitor friend, James L. Steele, John got a job with Inland Revenue as a Tax Inspector and later joined the law firm Norton Rose in London, where he is now head of their International Tax Department and a partner in the firm. He is happily married to Fiona, and they have two lovely children, Benjamin John who is now thirteen (1997) and Kate Elizabeth who is eleven. It was a great joy to us when we became grandparents. They live in a large house in its own grounds in Newport, Essex. We do wish it was nearer, for we'd love to see them more often, but are so thankful for being able to keep in touch on the telephone.

It is interesting to see the difference in our two sons.

Both brought up in the same home, both having the same pattern of education, but then so very different. John knew what he wanted to do and he pursued his career and quickly got established in a secure job.

Peter's travels

Peter was interested in journalism and was editor of the Arts section of The Courier, the University newspaper. This was a very time consuming job in addition to his studies. On leaving university, after a brief spell earning a bit of money, he decided, with a friend, to hitch hike across France and Spain to North Africa. From Morocco they went on a trip into the Sahara desert, having hitched a lift with a German couple. Unfortunately the extra weight of these two young men caused problems and they had to get out.

The Germans kindly waited until they got another lift. This time from a French couple who were heading back to Agadir in Morocco. The wife wasn't well and quickly got worse and by the time they reached Agadir had to be taken into hospital, where it was discovered that she had hepatitis. Peter and his friend decided to travel separately after this.

Foreign Office and International Red Cross to the rescue

We hadn't heard a word from Peter for almost two months, and then one Saturday morning the 'phone rang. It was the Foreign Office and I was asked if I had a son whose name was Peter Eric Challoner. I confirmed this, dreading what I was going to hear. It's amazing how so many things can crowd into the mind in such moments. He told me he had received a message from the British Embassy in Agadir to say that Peter was ill; that they had arranged for the International Red Cross to fly him home the next day and that he'd be arriving at Heathrow soon after 14.00 hrs. He also gave me the Red Cross number in London to get more details. We'll always be grateful for the help that we got during this time of crisis. On arrival at Heathrow an ambulance met him, prepared either to take him to hospital or bring him home, but Peter insisted that he was fit enough to travel by train. The ambulance driver 'phoned to make sure that we could meet him at Stoke. This we did and Peter arrived at 21.35 hrs. He looked ill but was amazingly cheerful. The doctor called in to see him the next morning and sent him at once to the Isolation Hospital at Bucknall where they confirmed that he had hepatitis. Thankfully he recovered in about two months, and was soon off on another adventure.

Teaching in Sudan

He applied for a job in the Sudan, after seeing an advert for an English teacher in a technical school in Nyala in West Sudan. He was accepted and went for a year but when he came home for a holiday, he announced that he was going back for a second year. He had fallen in love with these people. It's impossible for us to imagine what it was like to live in a place where the houses are built of mud and